THE BAGEL

"A fascinating and definitive account of the origins and importance in East European Jewish society of this boiled and baked ring of dough which has, surprisingly, become a staple item in the American diet."
—Antony Polonsky, Professor of Holocaust Studies, Brandeis University

"Maria Balinska combines stories, history and hands-on experience with a style as brisk and toothsome as the crust of a freshly baked bagel and content as dense and flavourful as its skilfully handled dough."
—Gillian Riley, author of *The Oxford Companion to Italian Food*

"This charming and highly informative book is a surprisingly delightful read, which strays into what seems a byway of history, but in which even readers without her background will find much that is not only amusing but of genuine historical interest."
—Joseph Frank, Professor Emeritus of Slavic and Comparative Literature, Stanford University

THE BAGEL
THE SURPRISING HISTORY OF A MODEST BREAD

MARIA BALINSKA

WITHDRAWN
UTSA LIBRARIES

Yale University Press
New Haven and London

A Caravan book. For more information, visit www.caravanbooks.org.

For information about this and other Yale University Press publications, please contact:

U.S. Office: sales.press@yale.edu   www.yalebooks.com
Europe Office: sales@yaleup.co.uk   www.yaleup.co.uk

Set in Minion by IDSUK (DataConnection) Ltd.
Printed in the United States of America.

Library of Congress Cataloging-in-Publication Data

Balinska, Maria.
   The bagel: the surprising history of a modest bread/Maria Balinska.
      p. cm.
   Includes bibliographical references.
   ISBN 978-0-300-11229-0 (ci: alk. paper)
   1. Bagels—History. 2. Jews, East European. I. Title.
   TX770.B35B35 2008
   641.8'15—dc22   2008026763

A catalogue record for this book is available from the British Library.
10 9 8 7 6 5 4 3 2 1

CONTENTS

LIST OF ILLUSTRATIONS

1 Baker shaping rings, photograph in *The Bakers' & Confectioners' Journal*, March 1950. From the Bakery, Confectionery and Tobacco Workers' International papers, Special Collections Department, University of Maryland Libraries.
2 Uigur woman selling *girde*. Mark Ralston/AFP/Getty Images.
3 'Tazzine di porcellana, limone su basamento, cocomero e ciambelle' by Cristoforo Munari. Musei di Strada Nuova, Palazzo Bianco, Genoa.
4 'Ritratto di Francesco Maria de' Medici bambino' by Giusto Suttermans. Galleria Palatina, Florence (Inv.1912 n.344), Soprintendenza Library.
5 Engraving of bakery from the *Kodeks Baltazara Bohema* (1505). Special Collections, Jagellonian Library, Kraków (rkp. BJ 16, k. 252v).
6 'Madonna della Pappa' by Lorenzo Lippi. Basilica di Santa Croce, Florence, Soprintendenza Library.
7 Cartoon of Jan Sobieski, Building 19 promotional leaflet.

ACKNOWLEDGEMENTS

I am grateful to many people for their help, support and advice.

At the beginning of the project, historian Dr Michael Berkowitz, food historians Susan Weingarten and Gillian Riley, Yiddish scholar Dr Helen Beer, novelist Sue Woolfe and fellow bagel writer Marilyn Bagel provided encouragement and valuable leads.

Lynn Kutner, baking instructor at the New School in New York, and British bread scientist Stanley Cauvain explained the complicated chemistry behind the bagel-making process.

In Puglia Comasia Vinci at Artevacanze went out of her way to introduce me to *tarallo* bakeries and the local food historian.

In Poland Kazimierz Czekaj, President of the Kraków Bakers' Guild, has been generous with information about the Guild and the *obwarzanek*. The historian Monika Polit helped with research at the Jewish Historical Institute in Warsaw. The musical director of Warsaw's Jewish Theatre, Teresa Wrońska, was indefatigable in chasing down various versions of the 'Bublitchki' song. Dr Michał

Kopczyński of Warsaw University explained the vicissitudes of wheat prices across the centuries. Photographer Jerzy Szot helped me find illustrative material.

Inevitably, I have spent a lot of time in libraries. Ilana Tahan of the British Library, Eleanor Yadin at the New York Public Library, Tammy Popejoy at the American Institute of Baking and archivist Vital Zajka at YIVO (the Yiddish Scientific Institute) all helped me find bagel-related material. I am particularly grateful to Jennie Levine who, as Curator for Historical Manuscripts at the University of Maryland's Hornbake Library, was responsible for one of my principal sources: the archives of the Bakery and Confectionery Workers' International.

In New York, journalist Sally Herships was an enthusiastic ally in tracking down information and people, and Muriel Hertan a welcoming host. Jocelyn Cohen and Daniel Soyer gave me access to their unpublished notes on the 1942 YIVO essay competition, thanks to which I came across Hyam Plumka, the bakery helper. And bakery owner David Teyf kindly allowed me to spend a very early morning in one of his bakeries to observe close up the process of making bagels.

I am grateful to all the former members of Bagel Bakers Union Local 338 who spoke to me; my especial thanks goes to Mike Edelstein, Stanley Katz, Terry Skolnick and Marvin Kralstein for their detailed descriptions of life in Local 338 in the 1950s and 1960s.

Marvin Lender, Willy Evans and Barry Ansel were welcoming and forthcoming about the history of Lender's Bagels.

In Mattoon, I was fortunate to be shown around by the town's unofficial historian Alice Larabee, the town's former mayor Roger Dettro and local journalist Janice Hunt.

In Montreal I received a crash course on the city's Jewish heritage from the Montreal Jewish Library's archivist Eiran Harris and journalist Leslie Lutsky.

In Australia Jacqueline Pascarl attended Melbourne's Yiddish Wednesday on my behalf and interrogated people there about their bagel memories. In London Matthew Reisz gave valuable editorial feedback and my colleagues at the BBC – Rosie Goldsmith, Arlene Gregorius, Tim Mansel, Hugh Levinson, Sian Glaessner – have given crucial help with translations and proffered an eclectic selection of bagel-related material from around the world.

There are three people in particular whose support was crucial to the writing of this book. I benefited hugely from the knowledge and enthusiasm of both Barry Davis, lecturer in Yiddish and Jewish history, and historian Dr Joanna Newman. Joanna was an exacting and encouraging editor of my first drafts. Finally, my husband (and first reader) Wojtek Szczerba may want no thanks, but it is to him that the greatest thanks are due. This book is dedicated to him and to my daughter Lucy Si Du.

NOTE TO READERS

I have chosen to adhere to English spelling conventions, as found in the Oxford English Dictionary. There are, inevitably, a number of exceptions. Quotations from American sources retain American spelling.

With the exception of the Polish capital Warsaw, I have spelled Polish names (for people and places) using the Polish alphabet.

What little Yiddish there is in the text could be spelled in a number of different ways. I have used the YIVO Library of Congress Transliteration System when citing in Yiddish. I have also chosen to refer to bagels from the very beginning as 'bagels' rather than 'beigels'. According to Yiddishists, the Lithuanian pronunciation of the Yiddish word would sound more like 'bagel' and the Galician more like 'beigel'. In the United States 'bagel' soon became the accepted anglicisation although it was only in 1964 that Local 338 of the Bakery and Confectionery Workers' International officially changed their name from the 'Beigel Bakers' to the 'Bagel Bakers'.

INTRODUCTION

Walking along the closest equivalent Warsaw has to New York's Fifth Avenue one bright spring morning, I spotted what looked like an artist's canvas on a tripod outside the elegant Blikle Café. Pavement advertising might be common in other European cities but Blikle was Warsaw's most famous and venerable pastry shop and such display seemed almost vulgar. But this was the early 1990s and Warsaw was changing at a blistering pace: maybe Blikle was too. Indeed, the Blikle display proudly announced the arrival of 'the New York breakfast' of smoked salmon, cream cheese and bagels. Expensive and exotic, the arrival of the New York branded bagel seemed to be just one more sign that borders really were coming down and that Poland was opening up to Western tastes.

At about the same time as Blikle launched its new menu, one of the many Americans who had come to Poland to 'teach capitalism' gave up his handsome management consultant's salary to open a bagel bakery. In Budapest, a young Harvard graduate used his bonus from an investment bank to start a restaurant chain called New York Bagel. Soon, the English-language press across Eastern Europe was publishing articles about where in Warsaw, Prague or Budapest one might find the 'best' bagel.

The irony, of course, is that far from being exotic, the bagel was, in fact, being reintroduced to its place of origin. Sixty years previously bagels were common in Warsaw, though as cheap street food rather than smart restaurant fare, available from the baskets of hundreds of bagel pedlars, the overwhelming majority of whom were Jewish.

The confident return of the bagel to Eastern Europe, not as a Jewish favourite but as the embodiment of an envied American way of life, is a story with obvious dramatic potential. It is the classic tale of the successful immigrant: his quest for acceptance and fortune and his triumph against the odds, a triumph leavened by the necessary compromises he has made in constructing a new identity for himself. The bagel emerges as an eloquent metaphor for the experience of Eastern European Jewry – and not just in America.

In America the bagel's path was essentially upwards. In the Old World, however, what began as an expensive product in seventeenth-century Poland by the 1930s had become a symbol of destitution: to be a bagel pedlar meant living in the most abject poverty. This does not mean that the bagel went uncelebrated in literature and art. Nor did it lose its widespread popularity within Poland. From the modest, everyday perspective of the bagel, it becomes clear that the Jews did not live in a 'world apart' as they have sometimes been portrayed. For all the suffering and prejudice that the Jewish community encountered in Poland over the centuries, the history of the bagel shows the degree to which Jewish culture was an integral part of the Polish landscape.

Today a new generation of historians – Polish, Israeli and American – is taking a more holistic approach to their study of Poland. They are aided in their task by the release of unexpected sources following the end of communism, as well as by the passing of time since the Holocaust. It is striking, for example, that Jewish Studies departments are thriving at Polish universities. The work of these historians is pioneering; it has certainly proved of great value to this book.

As to how I came to place such a burden of meaning on the unassuming bagel, it all started when I discovered a bagel equivalent – the *bajgiel* or *obwarzanek* – in the Polish city of Kraków in 1984. Having literally survived on bagels as a graduate student in Washington DC, I was missing them terribly in the ration-book Poland of communist General Jaruzelski where I spent a postgraduate year at the Jagellonian University, learning Polish and discovering my roots. After making the inevitable comparisons in taste and texture between bagel and *bajgiel*, I became intrigued as to what the connections were between the two breads. And over the years, as I investigated further, I came to understand that my own family history was relevant to that of the bagel. My father's family is Polish – part Jewish, part gentile. Both sides were actively involved in Polish public and cultural life. My Jewish great great grandfather founded the Warsaw Philharmonia; my Jewish great grandfather founded the Polish Institute of Hygiene; my gentile great grandfather was Leader of the Warsaw City Council and the author of a book about prewar

Warsaw; my gentile great uncle was one of the country's leading poets in the 1920s. They all doubtless frequented the Blikle Café as well as bought bagels from roadside pedlars, and they were all key players in the multicultural Poland encountered in this book.

On the other side of the Atlantic, my father was the wartime immigrant who became an American and raised his family in the greater New York area during the 1960s. We did not, however, have bagels at home. I ate my first bagel in a university canteen in the early 1980s. And it was green. Green for St Patrick's Day, thereby signalling (although I was not aware of it at the time) that the bagel was well on its way to becoming an all-American bread. Over the past twenty-odd years, my enthusiasm for eating bagels has not dimmed, even though I now live in Great Britain and (somewhat controversially for New York friends) laud the virtues of the bagels made in the Jewish bakeries of the London suburb of Golders Green.

So with my bagel credentials and motivations clearly on the table, it is time to define terms. The bagel, according to *Webster's Dictionary*, is 'a hard bread roll made of yeast dough, twisted into a small doughnut like shape, cooked in simmering water, then baked'. This is an admirably clear and concise description but it raises immediate questions. What makes a bread roll 'hard'? Why is the bagel ring-shaped? And why go to the trouble of boiling before baking? The search for answers to these questions has taken me to places – southern Italy and northern China – not usually linked with the bagel. What is clear is that the bagel has a host of possible ancestors – and most of them are not Jewish.

The next question is – why Poland? Why is it that, as Leo Rosten points out in his perennially popular *Joys of Yiddish*, the first mention of the word bagel, in a seventeenth-century Yiddish source, is recorded in the royal city of Kraków? And how did it come to pass that the most popular legend about the bagel, still regularly told, concerns a Polish king and his dramatic victory over the Turks at Vienna in 1683?

When I first started trawling through memoirs, newspapers, novels, songs and paintings for mentions and sightings of the bagel in Eastern European Jewish life, I wasn't sure what I'd find. There is, I admit, some bias to this research – most of my sources are Polish (both in Yiddish, read with the help of Yiddishists in London, New York and Warsaw, and in Polish). But with so much of European Jewry over the centuries having lived in what one might, for simplicity's sake, refer to as 'greater Poland', or in lands that were once Polish (which include much of today's Lithuania, Latvia, Belarus and Ukraine), it is a justifiable framework. And within that framework what begins to emerge first is that the bagel is a bread which, without being central to daily nutrition (as rye bread is in many areas) or to religion (as the sweet, plaited Sabbath challah is to Judaism), nevertheless has some special quality. The bagel will not be ignored: it pushes itself into the picture in the most unlikely places. Here it is, for example, in one of the stories told about the founder of Hassidism, the Ba'al Shem Tov, and there it is, half of it already inside a child's mouth, in the bottom corner of an oil painting of a nineteenth-century tavern scene. By the 1930s, the bagel was centre stage as various artists and writers used the story of the bagel and its pedlars to promote their vision of a better society.

The bagel arrived in America together with hundreds of Jewish bakers who were part of the massive wave of immigration into the United States between 1881 and 1914, and soon made its presence felt in Jewish immigrant literature. It played a part, too, in the long struggle to organise a lasting Jewish bakers' union, a union whose achievements have been overshadowed by the far larger story of the garment workers' movement. In 1937, the Bagel Bakers Union, Local 338 of the Bakery and Confectionery Workers' International Union, was founded in New York and until the late 1960s its members dominated bagel production in America. When technology caught up and a bagel machine was invented, it did so at the same time as Americans were opening their kitchens to so-called ethnic foods and their televisions to Jewish comedians. With supermarkets becoming central to food shopping, the time was right to launch the bagel nationwide. One family of bakers, the Lenders, jumped on the bandwagon and ended up as the country's first bagel millionaires. Now millions of bagels are consumed every day across the United States and sales are estimated to be worth over $900 million annually.

It is a special and curious story. The bagel, despite its modest stature, manages to bridge cultural divides, to rescue kings from relative obscurity, and to challenge received wisdoms. At the same time, the bagel is incapable of taking itself too seriously. Humour always lurks nearby. No biographer of the bagel can embark on this project without embracing the laughter and the affection which this bread inevitably inspires.

CHAPTER 1

THE FAMILY TREE

The landscape of the valley of Itria in Italy's 'heel', Puglia, could come straight out of the pages of a children's storybook with its gently rolling green hills and profusion of squat *trulli* or conical roofed houses. Dominating the valley from the top of one of its higher hills is the eighteenth-century town of Martina Franca. At first glance, its gleaming boutiques and noisy traffic do not seem particularly different from those of most Italian towns. And yet Martina has a certain timeless quality. The narrow streets are clean and tidy; the ornate baroque squares with their glistening marble paving stones are uncluttered by international brand names. There aren't many tourists about. Puglia, until recently at least, has been off the international beaten track.

One of the calling cards used by the marketing men and women in the past couple of years to promote Puglia has been its cooking. Puglia is in the country's wheat belt; it is from here that the hard durum wheat so prized by pasta-makers comes. It is also the home of a boiled and baked ring-shaped bread called the *tarallo*.

Look in the shop window of Martina Franca's bakeries and, if you are a bagel maven, you will do a double take. There, displayed invitingly in baskets, are what seem to be piles of bagel halves toasted until nut brown. On the shelves are stacked upright cellophane bags containing miniature bagels, labelled 'plain', 'fennel' and 'egg'. Walk from the shop front into the bakery proper and you will find the requisite freestanding kettle and a large sieve hanging on the tiled wall to scoop the *taralli* out of the water, drain them and carry them to the nearby oven. It all looks rather familiar to anyone who has visited bagel bakeries.

The bagel, in other words, may have family. Tracing the roots of putative antecedents can shed light on how the bagel was created. The stories of these far-flung cousins have something to say about how the bagel was originally made and consumed. By highlighting what makes its branch of the family tree distinct from that of other breads, we begin to give a shape to the bagel's unique identity.

* * *

In her classic compendium of Jewish cooking, the American writer Leah W. Leonard asserted that bagels (or, as she described them, 'water doughnuts') 'are as distinctly Jewish as Gefilte Fish'.[1] It is, however, a fact that ring-shaped boiled and baked breads like the *tarallo* are to be found across the world. We need, therefore, to take a closer look at the bagel's constituent parts. What distinguishes the bagel from, say, the Italian *tarallo*?

Flour is the starting point of any bread. The contemporary bagel's particular plasticity calls for a special kind, for wheat that is high in gluten. Comprised principally of protein, gluten is an elastic substance that the Chinese call 'the muscle of flour'.[2] Whether produced in New York City or London's East End, the modern bagel owes much of its chewiness to American wheat from the Dakotas and Kansas, which typically contains 14 per cent gluten compared to the 11 per cent gluten of ordinary bread flour. Combined with the relatively small amount of water in its dough,[3] this makes for a stiff, unyielding matter: tales of having to resort to kneading by foot are no exaggeration. So it is hardly surprising that the bagel beats most records for the speed at which it becomes stale. 'Cement doughnut' and 'jawbreaker' are not just figures of speech. A traditionally made bagel is past its prime after a mere five hours.

Taralli, in contrast, are intended to be hard – and long lasting. They were the bread of choice for pilgrims and traders travelling by land or sea. Mentioned, for example, in a 1397 document about ships and international trade, they were prized as a non-perishable food that could be stored in the hull, transported over long distances and eaten many weeks after they were made.[4] Today's *taralli* are advertised as 'good for' six months – and that is without any chemical preservative. Like a thick cracker, they crumble easily in the mouth: the flour of southern Italy is low in gluten. In the fourteenth century the *tarallo*'s hardness was probably more akin to that of hard-tack, and could only be softened by dedicated chewing or – just as day-old bagels a few centuries later – by dunking in hot liquid.

In Puglia, the *taralli* that tourists are now offered to accompany their glass of wine began life, as far as we know, in medieval Italy. The word comes from the early Italian '*tar*', to bend around and enclose. It is this ring shape which has made the *tarallo*, like the bagel, such a distinctive foodstuff. For the bakers of *taralli*, it was a shape which presented various practical and symbolic advantages without creating major production difficulties. The *tarallo's* low gluten dough was relatively easy to roll. It was a different story for the bagel, whose stiff, recalcitrant dough would prove a stumbling block for everyone who attempted to mechanise the ring-shaping process. In the days before the machine the 'rollers' were the kings of the bagel team, using a technique that requires great dexterity and takes months to perfect. From a large mound of dough the rollers cut off a slab and roll it with both hands into a long uniform rope. Then with one hand they break off a sausage-shaped piece about 6 inches long and, winding it round that hand's four fingers, solder the ends together with a few deft flicks of the hand against the table. A good 'roller' needs no more than a few seconds to shape each bagel.

The traditional bagel prides itself on its full flavour and thick shiny crust, culinary glories achieved by 'retarding' the dough rings by keeping them in a cool place for a certain length of time (up to twenty hours) prior to cooking. Retardation slows down the fermentation process caused by yeast and instead encourages the formation of lactic acid bacteria, naturally found in yeast but usually undeveloped in warm doughs. What their greater presence gives the bagel is more flavour or, as one bread scientist has put it, 'a slightly acid bite'.[5] It is also thanks to retardation that the bagel acquires its substantial crust. A much reduced cooling period, according to a laboratory experiment carried out at the University of Kansas, results in a 'pale crust and a texture

1. Rollers shape bagel rings in 1950s' America.

[lacking] the chewy-tough characteristics of a traditional bagel'.[6] A standard procedure in the repertoire of today's baker, retardation is thought to have been introduced simply because bakers were either unwilling or unable to work through the night. (For the bakers of *taralli*, this step is of little interest because there is no yeast in *tarallo* dough).

What both breads do have in common, however, is the process of boiling before baking. In the *tarallo*'s case, boiling was a later refinement to the original recipe, an innovation that allowed the baker to make bigger rings without losing their shape. The same principle holds true for the bagel: once it is boiled it retains its shape in the oven. Cooking the surface of the dough in water also gelatinises the starch and creates the distinctive glossy crust. For bagel aficionados, the act of boiling is invested with near mythical status because of its importance and its trickiness. Boil the bagel for too long – over a minute say some, over two minutes say others – and the dough will collapse; boil it for too short a time and the dough will not expand and the finished product will be very dense and very hard.

And so to the oven. The bagels are scooped out of the kettle with a wire basket and arranged in a row on oblong boards of wood or 'peels' covered with burlap. Now the rings are glistening and white, shrinking at the touch. Some bakers give the rolls a moment to dry before putting them in the oven. Others cool them down with cold water. Either way, the oven the bagels subsequently enter is set at a higher temperature than the usual bread oven. Half way through the baking the baker, in another skilled and physically demanding move, flips the ten bagels over on to the oven shelf and pulls out the peel. After at most half an hour the bagels are lifted out of the oven on a big paddle and deposited in a basket, ready to be consumed.

For all their differences, the similarities between the bagel and the *tarallo* hint at a shared and venerable heritage. What, then, makes the bagel Jewish?

* * *

Ring-shaped breads have a long pedigree on the Italian peninsula, a region which from Roman times has had a profound
cultural and culinary impact on the rest of Europe. The twice-
baked circular *buccellatum* was a staple food for the soldiers of the
Roman Empire,[7] and as such would have travelled by the wagon
load across Europe and the lands around the Mediterranean. In its
turn, this Roman bread may well have been the inspiration for the
first Christians' communion bread which was made of wheat (this
despite diverging opinions as to whether Jesus himself would have
eaten what was then expensive wheat bread at the Last Supper),
ring-shaped and large enough for the entire congregation to
share.[8] Although this wreath-shaped bread would give way to the
much smaller communion wafer, many monasteries continued to
bake lean dough rings (without fat, eggs or sugar) as a special
fasting bread for Lent. In time this skill was passed on to lay
craftsmen. In the *tarallo*'s case any specific connotations of abstinence, however, seem to have disappeared.

The Roman *buccellatum* may also have inspired the Arab *kak*,
a ring-shaped biscuit sweetened with honey and dried fruits,
spiced with cinnamon and hard baked to last for months. *Kak*
was eaten across the Middle East and even merits a mention in
the Talmud.[9] It also probably accompanied Arab traders to the
busy Puglian port of Bari.

Bari was the principal embarkation point for the crusades and
the main port for the shipping of local wheat. It was a meeting
place for Christian pilgrims, Jewish scholars and traders of all
backgrounds – Arab, Christian and Jewish. Along with Rome,

ninth-century Puglia was home to the Italian peninsula's most important Jewish community. Today the town of Oria, a two-hour drive inland from Bari, is sleepy and ostentatiously Catholic, but in the ninth century it was a renowned centre of Jewish learning and a magnet for scholars who travelled from as far afield as Jerusalem and Baghdad to study there.[10]

Although the Jewish presence in Puglia came to a shuddering halt in the sixteenth century with the Spanish conquest of the region and the extension of the Catholic regime's Inquisition, there are a number of local customs that continue to be attributed to Jewish influence. From the outlines of a menorah (the eight-branched candelabrum lit during the festival of Channukah) on the whitewashed roofs of stone houses to the chicory soup eaten on Easter Monday and the artichoke omelette that is a local speciality, 'vague traces of Jewish beliefs and practices', the eminent historian Cecil Roth concluded in his *History of the Jews of Italy*, 'are to be discerned ... in southern Italy'. For a good many centuries Jewish artisans and traders as well as scholars lived fairly harmoniously side by side with their non-Jewish neighbours. Could Jewish bakers have been making *taralli*? Food historians in Puglia do not dismiss the connection.

But could the Jewish identity of the ring-shaped bread have been cemented even further east? The evidence for a potential Chinese connection is the golden circular bread called the *girde,* which is still baked today by the Muslim Uigurs of north-western China. The *girde,* which has an indentation rather than a hole at its centre, is cooked in a variety of ways, although many accounts describe a process not dissimilar to that of bagel making with the dough being

2. A Uigur mother and son sell *girde* in Xianjiang Province, China.

steamed as well as baked.[11] Contemporary and historical descriptions of eating *girde* certainly confirm similarities of consistency as well as appearance: 'it lay like a stone on the stomach' commented one traveller. Just like the *tarallo* and the bagel, when the *girde* gets old and stale it also is commonly dipped in hot tea or soup to soften it.

And just like the *tarallo* with its ready access to the rest of Europe through the port of Bari, the *girde* (or, more accurately, its ancestor) was being made on one of the greatest of trading highways, the Silk Route. There are many accounts of Jewish traders from Europe travelling this lengthy journey. Would they have brought home recipes for the foods they encountered and enjoyed in northern China? There are no written records to support this romantic theory. Just as Italian pasta has been shown to predate Marco Polo's Chinese travels, so the *girde* and its ancestors probably have no more in common with the bagel than the cheering fact that, presented with similar ingredients, human beings have a tendency to create similar products.

What we do know is that by the sixteenth century ring-shaped wheaten bread was being eaten the length and breadth of the Italian peninsula. Recipe books from the period show that *brazatelle* (from the Italian for bracelet) and *ciambelle* were being boiled, baked and eaten in Tuscan convents and in the noble courts of the city of Ferrara. The increasing affordability of wheat, thanks, among other things, to grain imports from Eastern Europe, encouraged new recipes and abstemiousness was no longer a defining factor. In the Dominican convent of San Tommaso in Perugia, Sister Maria Vittoria della Verde made 'drowned *ciambelle*' from flour, yeast, salt, sugar and anise seeds.[12] In Ferrara, Christofaro di Messisbugo, the steward at the Duke of Este's court, noted down the recipe for *brazzatelle di latte* which consisted of flour, rose water, milk, sugar, eggs and butter; they were to be boiled in water until they rose to the surface, scooped up, rinsed in fresh water and then baked.[13]

These different ring breads were very much part of people's everyday lives. The early modern marketplace was always full of *ciambella* vendors, hawking their wares from specially constructed baskets with spikes in them. As wheat became more widely available and affordable, *ciambelle* were a sensible as well as a tasty choice, as the verse under the seventeenth-century engraving of one pedlar suggests:

Buying *ciambelle* is a good habit
Aniseed, oil, butter and eggs
It doesn't just make the food go further
The buyer finds it an economy.[14]

At the same time, *ciambelle* were also depicted served on fine bone china plates gracing the tables of the prosperous citizens of Perugia and Florence alongside such luxury items as drinking chocolate, silverware and game. From the bustling marketplace to the elegant dining room, *ciambelle* were aided in their social mobility by coming in a variety of recipes, making them available at a variety of prices. But the ease with which they crossed class barriers indicates that they had an appeal which went beyond the ordinary.

Ciambelle were a treat, not a staple and as such had a particular appeal for children, as indeed the bagel and its other cousins would

3. One of Cristoforo Munari's (1667–1720) many still-lifes of *ciambelle.*

too. Sweet *ciambelle* had an especial attraction, but the shape of the rolls – easy to grip, bite into and play with – made them irresistible. In the seventeenth-century portrait of three-year-old Prince Francesco Maria de' Medici, the little boy is shown dressed in silken splendour in front of a sumptuous red curtain, a *ciambella* clutched firmly in his left hand. Was this the bribe exacted, one wonders, to persuade him to stand on a pedestal to be painted? Even the baby Jesus is given a *ciambella* to hold in the Florentine painter Lorenzo Lippi's *Madonna della pappa*, a picture emphasising the human bond between mother and son and indicating the trend for contemporary artists to depict the holy family in a more naturalistic way. The *ciambella* also serves to echo the halo above Jesus's head. Both ring-shaped, one perfect the other imperfect; both with no beginning and no end. In religious terms they are intimations of eternity; in folklore their connotations were magical.

4. Francesco Maria de' Medici poses for his portrait with *ciambella* in hand.

In most cultures, round objects are associated with good luck. A bread with no beginning and no end has a certain charmed quality. In Puglia to give one's friend or neighbour *taralli* was to wish them good luck and prosperity. Hardly surprising then that an amicable end to a squabble came to be summed up by the expression '*tutto finisce a tarallucci e vino*' (everything ends up with *tarallucci* and wine).

With such positive connotations and practical advantages, was the *ciambella* an item that Jewish traders might have consumed on the road, or students from Poland (among them Jewish students of medicine) might have taken as gifts when finishing their studies in Padua or Ferrara? Certainly the *ciambella* was a foodstuff that the young Italian noblewoman who became Queen of Poland in 1518 would have wanted to have continued to eat in her new home. Bona Sforza, who came from the Puglian port of Bari, arrived in the Polish royal city of Kraków with a retinue of over three hundred Italians, including her Neapolitan cook. She delighted in lavish cuisine and was instrumental in introducing a number of spices to her new subjects. It is indeed in Kraków that we find the first recorded reference to the Jewish bagel – but Poland had been producing a bagel-like bread, the *obwarzanek*, for over a hundred years before Queen Bona's arrival.

* * *

The first mention of the *obwarzanek* dates from 1394 and is to be found in the accounts of the Polish royal household.[15] The bread was made specifically for Jadwiga, arguably the most popular of Poland's queens. Jadwiga, whose marriage to the Lithuanian

Duke Jagietto created the Polish Lithuanian Commonwealth, was known for her charity and her piety. During Lent, for example, she would wear a hair shirt, and evidently eat *obwarzanki*. For the *obwarzanek* (or *obarzanek*; both words derive from the verb *obwarzyć*, to parboil) was a lean bread, made without fat and therefore appropriate fare for Lent or any other fast day. It was also probably made of wheat flour, if not wholly then at least partially. In an area of Europe where rye was the dominant grain, this made the *obwarzanek* a luxury food despite its association with abstinence. It was, in other words, a Lenten bread fit for the royal table.

It is likely that the *obwarzanek* (which is also referred to in Polish documents by the Latin word *circulis*) reached Poland via Germany. Medieval Poland was a land of peasants and noblemen, with a pressing need for artisans and traders. In order to develop the country's nascent urban economy, Poland's princes made deliberate efforts to attract skilled migrants from the West so that by the fifteenth century Kraków was renowned for its German-speaking burghers and artisans.[16] It was in Germanic lands that the ring-shaped communion bread used by the early Christians first left the confines of the monastery and developed into the feast day bread which would come to be known as the pretzel. As pretzel historian Irene Krauss has shown, the shape of this wheaten bread evolved from a circle to a three-holed oblong which is said to be modelled on the outline of a monk's arms in prayer.[17] There is little doubt that this special bread – a symbol of good luck and good health and offered, like the *tarallo*, as a gift – accompanied the eastward-bound Germans to Polish cities.

5. Making *obwarzanki* in Kraków in the sixteenth century. Note the 'kettle' to the right of the oven.

Germans, however, were not the only immigrants to Kraków in the Middle Ages. Poland's kings also encouraged Jewish craftsmen and traders to set up shop in their royal city, most of whom came to Kraków from German towns. They, too, may have arrived with a version of the pretzel or bagel already part of their baking repertoire. There are, indeed, references to pretzels in thirteenth-century Jewish documents and expert opinion concurs that the word bagel comes from the Yiddish *beigen*, to bend, which in turn is related to *bouc*, the word with the same meaning in Middle High German. According to one now seldom-told folk tale, the bagel's birthplace was an 'out of the way corner of Prussia' in the ninth century. Such was the religious fervour of the time, goes the story, that many Christians insisted that any kind of bread, given its connection with the person of Jesus Christ, should be denied Jews. The Christian mob began attacking any Jew who had the temerity to continue to buy or bake bread. However, the local ruler was a wise man and, having been petitioned by the local Jewish community,

announced that it had been ruled that only what was *baked* could be properly called bread. The Jews promptly took the hint and departed to seek out a way to prepare wheat without baking. What they decided on was boiling and what resulted was the first batch of bagels ever made. In the beginning the boiled product was only 'toasted' a little; gradually, however, when things had quietened down, it began to be both boiled and baked.[18]

The folk tale does not say whether this new bread creation was eaten by the gentiles of this 'out of the way corner of Prussia'. In

Poland, the ruling princes were certainly not against Jewish bakers offering their wares to all buyers. The privileges drawn up by Prince Bolesław the Pious in 1264 to establish the Jews' legal status in their new home seem to make a special dispensation for bakers: 'we resolve,' says article 36, 'that Jews may freely buy and sell everything and touch bread like Christians'. This was a radical step, so radical that in 1267 a group of Polish bishops forbade Christians to buy any foodstuffs from Jews, darkly hinting that they contained poison for the unsuspecting gentile. The proclamation of such a ban itself indicates that the products of Jewish artisans were indeed finding favour among Christian consumers.

When the bagel came into being in Poland, it had competition in the form of the *obwarzanek*. This is the family link which would have the defining influence on the fate of the bagel. In a land of rye, both breads were highly prized and their production was regulated by their respective communities. The first document to mention the bagel is a 1610 sumptuary law, a law whose purpose is to restrain expenditure. As we shall see, the Jewish Elders of Kraków were particular in their instructions on just when bagels should be consumed and by whom. Among gentiles, the *obwarzanek* continued to be eaten, especially during Lent. Some two hundred years after Queen Jadwiga's death, in 1611 the Bakers' Guild of Kraków officially decreed the *obwarzanek* a Lenten bread that could only be baked by selected bakers. The bagel's circumstances, in other words, were very different to that of the *tarallo* or the *ciambella*, at least at first. Although it would later become an ubiquitous market bread, beloved of jokesmiths and children, the bagel began life as a bread of value and an object of respect.

6. Bagel echoes halo in Lorenzo Lippi's *Madonna della Pappa*.

CHAPTER 2

OF BAGELS AND KINGS

According to legend, the bagel was produced as a tribute to Jan Sobieski, King of Poland, who had just saved Austria from an onslaught by Turkish invaders. In gratitude, a local baker shaped yeast dough into the shape of a stirrup to honor him and called it a 'beugel' (Austrian for stirrup). The roll was a hit and it's [sic] shape soon evolved into the one we know today and it's [sic] name converted to 'Bagel'.

'History of Bagels' handout, Boston
area supermarket Building 19

It would not be surprising if, on his death bed, Jan Sobieski, King of Poland, had hoped that he would be remembered by posterity for his magnificent defeat of the Turks in Vienna in 1683. What he might have found puzzling, however, is how his name and his victory have become an enduring part of bagel folklore, so much so that they now figure in the promotional literature of an American supermarket chain in the Yankee stronghold of Boston.

7. Just one example of how Poland's King Jan Sobieski has been immortalised in bagel folklore.

The pairing of a Polish warrior king and a small Jewish bread roll is not only incongruous but is also entirely fictitious. Written evidence of the bagel's existence in Poland seventy-three years before the Battle of Vienna and nineteen years before Sobieski's birth proves the story is false. But that is not to say that it is insignificant. Polish kings in general and this Polish king in particular play significant parts in the bagel's story and in the story of the Jewish community who made this bread their own.

*   *   *

From as early as the seventh century Jews were living in the lands which would come to constitute Poland, but it was only from the twelfth century that they began to arrive from Western Europe in substantial numbers. For the Jewish community the pull of pastures new was enhanced by the push of the increasing precariousness of life in Germany and France. There, Christian guilds were making life impossible for Jewish artisans and traders, and Jews had to a large degree been relegated to the occupation of money-lending. A hostile Church fulminated against the Jewish religion and Jews became the scapegoat for all manner of calamities, most notably for the devastating Black Plague of 1348–9, during which hundreds of innocent Jews were murdered. Scores of German cities threw their Jewish inhabitants out altogether. The general consensus among the Jews of Northern Europe at this time was that life was safer under the protection of the Polish kings.

The official safeguards offered by the rulers of Poland were designed to reassure the new Jewish inhabitants that they could go about their business in safety while also enjoying the freedom to practise their religion and set up their own autonomous communal structures. In the first of these documents, the Statute of Kalisz of 1264, Prince Bolesław the Pious shows his awareness of the potential for communal tension. 'We resolve,' reads article 35, 'that if a Jew in an extreme predicament is forced to cry out in the night and his Christian neighbours do not attend to give him help then every neighbouring Christian will owe a payment of thirty soldos.'

When, in the fourteenth century, the discrete Polish principalities were united in the Kingdom of Poland, the privileges as outlined by Bolesław became the basis for the legal relationship between the Jewish community and the crown. King Kazimierz III established the precedent by extending the Kalisz privileges to Jews across his new realm, which he doubled in size during the course of his reign. The only Polish monarch to have the soubriquet 'great' attached to his name, Kazimierz has legendary status in Jewish folklore, credited (erroneously) with having been the first to bring Jews to Poland and believed to have fallen in love with a beautiful Jewish woman, Esterka, and had four children by her. There is no evidence to support this romantic liaison but its existence is a sign of the verifiable fact that Kazimierz relied on a number of Jews in his court, as indeed would most of Poland's kings.

Within the walls of the royal city of Kraków, however, Jews still encountered Christian antagonism. Confrontations were fuelled by the fiery rhetoric of a succession of Catholic clerics. Moreover, as home to one of Central Europe's oldest universities, Kraków was a hothouse of religious polemic and an entry point for European anti-Jewish literature. The potent message of these clerics – that the Jew was a dangerous economic rival, increasing his wealth at the expense of his Christian neighbour – resonated keenly with many of Kraków's merchants and artisans, whose campaign to close down their Jewish competition reached a climax in the summer of 1494.

The trigger was a fire which swept through the town one June evening, burning down houses, churches and many of the city's gates. It started, so the Kraków City Council alleged, in a Jewish baker's oven. Over the next few days Jewish shops were pillaged and one Jew died trying to defend his property. By September, most Jews had moved out of Kraków to the nearby city of

8. From 1494 Kazimierz (Casmiru) became the new centre of Kraków's Jewish community.

Kazimierz, leaving behind homes, synagogues, a public bath and a hospital the traces of which have all but disappeared.[1]

Kazimierz (which had been founded by and named after King Kazimierz III) was, however, very near, so near that despite its autonomous status it was generally considered to be part of what one might call 'greater' Kraków. It was, therefore, easy for Jewish merchants and artisans to continue to ply their trades back in Kraków where there was still demand for their goods and services, a turn of events that was looked upon none too kindly by their Christian competitors. The Kraków Bakers' Guild, for one, was acutely conscious of any bakers from outside the city walls. In 1496, just one year after the Jews left Kraków, King Jan Olbracht signed a decree that white bread and *obwarzanek* could be made and sold only by members of the Guild.[2] Such an edict would only have been necessary only if non-Guild *obwarzanek* (and, one assumes, non-gentile bagels) were undercutting sales.

* * *

In fact, despite the daily frustrations of dealing with Christian guilds, the sixteenth century and the first half of the seventeenth century would prove a golden age for Poland's Jews, and indeed for Poland generally. From a difficult start, Poland's economy had blossomed. The reason for this transformation was one commodity and one alone: grain.

Western Europe was looking for cheaper sources of grain; Poland with its expanse of fertile wide plains, particularly in the south-east, could oblige. For a century and a half Poland would be one of Europe's principal breadbaskets, its cereal reaching as far as

Portugal and Cyprus. Most of that cereal was rye but there were also oats and, when the harvests were plentiful, wheat. It comes as no surprise, therefore, to find in this period of plentiful grain the first written evidence of the existence of the Jewish bagel.

The cultivation of grain brought prosperity to the Jewish community. Enterprising noblemen who wanted to develop their farming estates needed to borrow money, so they turned to Jewish bankers. Jewish traders who knew how to deal with international customers were at a premium. Other Jewish merchants were able to make a handsome living from importing into Poland more expensive goods such as citrus fruits and wine, now desirable and affordable for noblemen flush with grain money. And in the east of the country, in what is now Ukraine, Jewish administrators were being hired by noble magnates to run their vast agricultural estates, newly established to meet Western demand for Polish cereal. The Jewish population in the east increased accordingly. From the mid-sixteenth to the mid-seventeenth century, the number of Jewish residents expanded more than tenfold.[3]

Most importantly, at this time Poland could offer its Jewish inhabitants peace and safety – in marked contrast to the rest of Europe. This had much to do with the country's distinctive system of government. The Kingdom of Poland–Duchy of Lithuania, the largest country in Europe, united formally under one parliament (or *sejm*) and one king in 1569. But this was a king like no other in Europe: he did not inherit the throne but was elected to it by the noblemen of Poland. An astonishing innovation in an age of hereditary monarchy, it was intro-duced because of the lack of a male heir. The establishment of a democratic vote sent out a strong message: the power of the monarch was not absolute. While other kings in Europe were busy centralising their authority, in Poland power was being devolved. This was the nobility's moment of glory. Their strength lay in their numbers and in their rural way of life. Unlike their French counterparts, for example, the Poles were less amenable to royal diktat for the simple reason that they spent very little time at the royal court. Uniquely in Europe there was a formalised balance of power in Poland. One political writer of the time boasted: '[other countries] have the riches of copper, gold and silver while [the Polish nation] considers its genuine freedom to be its greatest treasure'.[4]

The strength of Poland's nobility made for a weaker central state but a more tolerant society. While other Europeans were killing one another in the Reformation and then the Counter-Reformation, in Poland noblemen were peacefully converting to Calvinism (another means of proving their independence from the king), marriages between different faiths were not unheard of, and only one person was burnt at the stake. 'Heretics' from across Europe flocked to Poland, attracted by what one of its detractors called 'its devilish freedom of conscience'.[5] The towns and cities of Poland were the setting for a cacophony of languages and a wide variety of physical features, with their Italian anti-Trinitarians, German Lutherans and English Quakers mingling with the local Catholics, Russian Orthodox, Tartar Muslims and Jews.

Compared with England, France and Spain where 'much Israelite blood has been shed without the slightest reason',

Poland, wrote the Karaite[6] scholar Isaac ben Abraham Troki in 1594, treated its Jewish inhabitants well:

> . . . here Jews are even assisted with favourable privileges so that they can live happily and peacefully. The kings of these lands and their officials are lovers of magnanimity and righteousness and do not do the Jews living here any harm or wrong which is why God granted this land such great power and peace so that different faiths do not breathe hatred towards one another and do not condemn one another.[7]

Poland's particular political structure was ideal for the development of an autonomous Jewish life within Polish society. The Jews had their own councils and court system. They chose their own chief rabbi whose authority was recognised and enforced (on pain of death) by the king. Like other subjects of the realm, the Jews regularly paid taxes to the royal treasury but these taxes were collected by Jewish officials, not representatives of the king. The royal court was regularly frequented by Jewish bankers (most useful during expensive military campaigns), merchants, jewellers and doctors. Indeed, the Jewish community in Polish lands was becoming known across Europe for its scholars, its wealth and its standing. Poland was, as the popular seventeenth-century proverb put it, 'paradise for the Jews, hell for the peasants and heaven for the nobility'. But not for much longer.

In 1648 embittered Cossack noblemen led by Bohdan Khmielnytsky launched an uprising of murderously resentful peasants against the Polish landlords in the southeast of the country. As the landlords' agents, or the people with whom the peasants had the most regular contact, Jews were especial targets of the marauding gangs. The massacres were widespread and the violence savage: tens of thousands of Jews were killed. This marked the beginning of a period so disastrous that it came to be referred to as 'the Deluge'. From the east the Russians attacked; from the north the Swedes. There was an outbreak of plague. As battles raged across Polish territory, the grain trade was devastated and with it Poland's economy, which would not recover for two centuries. The civilian population was decimated. Whole cities were destroyed. Tolerance was eroded as an atmosphere of suspicion and fear descended on Polish lands. Jews became the target of blood libels, falsely accused of murdering gentile children in order to use their blood during the Passover ritual – accusations that were entirely without foundation. Poland had become, in the words of one Jewish poet, Moses of Narol, 'a widow, abandoned by her own sons'.[8] For the first time Jews began to leave Poland for Western Europe in significant numbers.

Internal peace was restored in 1656 but the damage was done. The golden age of Poland's grain trade, and the 'paradise' it had offered its Jewish inhabitants, was destroyed. Poland and its Jews were in dire need of a hero. That they found one in Jan Sobieski is fortunate; that he would be honoured with a bread roll requires a little more imagination.

*   *   *

Born in 1629, Jan Sobieski was the embodiment of the seventeenth-century Polish magnate. Generous, impetuous, wedded to the knightly virtues of honour and hospitality, Sobieski was a son of south-eastern Poland where his family had been granted land in return for their service on the battlefield. He, too, was expected to follow in their military footsteps. At the same time, he was aware that the economic fortunes of his family – and therefore his career – depended to a large extent on the Jewish administrators of his vast estates and the Jewish population of the towns which his fore-bears had established on these estates.

Sobieski cut his military teeth during the Deluge, fighting against Russians, Ukrainians and Swedes, as well as fellow Poles. By the age of twenty-seven he had risen to be one of the country's foremost military commanders. Poland was now at peace but the hostilities had left it weakened and its borders ill-defended, a fact that the Turks began to exploit in the 1670s. As strategically important towns and noble estates fell to the Ottoman troops, Commander Sobieski prepared for war. Lulled into complacency by the poor Polish defence of years past, the Turks were taken by surprise by the blow that Jan Sobieski dealt them one bitterly cold day in November 1673. The Ottoman troops were annihi-lated: of the 30,000 Turkish soldiers who woke up in the fortress town of Chocim on 10 November only 4,000 survived to see the morning of the 11th. Such was Sobieski's tactical brilliance that it would be fêted two hundred years later by no less a military expert than Carl von Clausewitz.

With the death of Poland's reigning monarch the night before the Chocim victory, the triumphant Sobieski was suddenly thrust forward as a candidate for the throne. The favourite that year was a foreigner, Carl of Lorraine, but the mood among the thousands of noblemen gathered to vote for the new monarch in a field outside Warsaw dictated that the new king should be Polish.

As the king of Poland and the victor of Chocim, forty-five-year old Jan Sobieski was already becoming a well-known figure across Europe. And how very different he looked from the powdered and bewigged monarchs of the West with their lace neckwear, fussy jackets and stockings. Sobieski made a point of dressing in what was then known as the 'Polish style', a style so distinctive that his Irish doctor, Bernard Connor, 'thought an account of it would not be unacceptable':

> They have all their hair cut round about their ears like monks and wear furr'd caps, large whiskers and no neckcloths; a long coat hangs down to their heels, and a waistcoat under that of the same length tied close about the waist with a girdle . . . instead of shoes they always wear both abroad and at home Turkey leather boots with very thin soles, and hollow deep heels made of a blade of Iron bent hoopwise into the form of a half moon.[9]

The 'Polish style' may have been mocked by the denizens of the French court in Versailles (where it was used as fancy dress for masked balls), but the French ambassador to Warsaw along with the rest of the diplomatic corps was soon making the long trip south-east to pay their respects to the new king at his favourite palace in the town of Żółkiew.

Named after its founder, Sobieski's grandfather, Stanisław Żółkiewski, Żółkiew had a substantial and prosperous Jewish community. From the very beginning of its existence, the town's owners had used their power to foster its economic growth not only by encouraging local trade but also by promoting religious co-existence.[10] The lesson that greater tolerance could engender greater prosperity was not lost on Sobieski, a man always keenly aware of the state of his coffers.

Today Żółkiew is the small, sleepy town of Zhovkva in Ukraine. The royal palace is a municipal building. The pink synagogue, built with a loan from Jan Sobieski, is empty and unused. But in the seventeenth century Żółkiew was famous across Poland and beyond. Foreign visitors wrote about its prominence

9. The pink Synagogue in Żółkiew in a nineteenth-century engraving by Jan Matejko.

and of the well-appointed homes of its Jewish residents. Indeed, the house pointed out by Sobieski himself as the model to be followed by all was that of his Jewish factor, Jakub Becal. Becal, who rose to become the administrator of royal customs, was a controversial figure. Despite the resentment he provoked among the Polish nobility, Sobieski steadfastly defended Becal at no insignificant cost to himself and his family. Portrayed in one caricature of the time with pockets bulging from the money provided by Becal,[11] Sobieski became an object of ridicule and his stubborn association with Becal may well have undermined his son's chances of being elected the next king.

The fact that Sobieski 'energetically defended Jews and surrounded himself with them from a young age',[12] as the leading Polish-Jewish historian Majer Bałaban put it, does not mean, however, that he treated his Christian and Jewish subjects as equals. Ever the pragmatist, Sobieski upheld a number of Christian guilds' requests for monopolies. Nor did he revoke the *de non tolerandis Judaeis* statutes which banned Jews altogether from certain cities. But the overall balance was positive, especially in light of what was to come. In the wake of the devastation wrought by years of war, Poland needed its Jews and it needed them to be working. Sobieski's reasoning is plain to see, for example, in his decree giving Jews the right to trade in the town of Piotrków:

Having taken into consideration the desolation of our cities and towns – and wanting to return them through Our Royal providence to their former perfection, so that they could have the benefit of trade, of people who are so skilled in trade.[13]

Furthermore, Sobieski took action to protect this right and ensure the physical safety of Jewish traders and artisans across Poland, his intervention in Kraków's 'great student riot' of 1682 being the most prominent example.

Angry at the alleged sale of stolen church silver by a Jewish trader, students and townspeople armed with sticks, swords and axes began looting Jewish shops. In the ensuing chaos, one of the Jewish merchants grabbed a rifle and fired a shot into the crowd. One young boy fell. The crowd went wild and the town was in uproar. Once the king learned of the riot he took matters into his own hands. Outraged by the behaviour of the students he focused his ire first on the university's rector and professors and then on the local authorities, informing them that he was rescinding their autonomy and establishing his own commission of inquiry in order to identify and punish the guilty. The commission dealt severely with the riot's student ringleaders sentencing one of them to death while Sobieski personally remitted the debts of the Jewish merchants whose merchandise had been ruined during the looting. Sobieski would be the last Polish king to protect his Jewish subjects in this way.

Acceding to the throne after the Deluge and preceding a period of painful economic and political decline, Sobieski would have been accorded a place in Jewish cultural memory had he displayed even a modicum of goodwill towards his Jewish subjects. In hindsight his reign would be seen as the last gasp of

Poland's golden age and he himself a figure to be yearned for. In Yiddish the expression '*in meylekh Sobieskis yorn*' ('in King Sobieski's time') became synonymous with the good old days. Over two hundred years after his death, Sobieski would be the hero of a poem telling the story of how, as the adopted son of a Jewish father, he was taught the Talmud before becoming king.[14] In Żółkiew, another legend had it that Sobieski was working as an errand boy in a Jewish household when one day the rabbi came to visit and saw a halo over the little boy's head. 'He is a godly person,' said the rabbi and fed and cleaned him. Later, the story concludes, that little boy became king and built the synagogue in Żółkiew by way of thanks.[15]

The Jewish community of Żółkiew had special reasons to be grateful to Jan Sobieski. But so did the Jewish bakers of Kraków. Sobieski was the first king *not* to confirm the decree issued by Jan Olbracht back in 1496 limiting the production of white bread and *obwarzanek* to the Kraków Bakers' Guild. Bagels, in other words, could now be sold inside the city walls. Sobieski's connection to the bagel is thereby confirmed. It is not, however, a particularly exciting tale. What is needed is a heroic narrative.

* * *

The Battle of Vienna of 1683 is a seminal moment in the confrontation between Christianity and Islam: the victory that turned back Ottoman ambitions in Europe forever. The significance of this event has been invoked by public figures on many occasions through the centuries, most recently during the debates over whether Turkey should become a member of the

European Union. It has also been commemorated by no fewer than three separate food legends – the bagel's included. The fact that this battle should have done so is testament not only to its geopolitical importance but also to the dramatic and compelling story of how the battle was won.

It was into a decidedly unsettled Central Europe – decimated by the Thirty Years War, its once fertile fields abandoned – and with Louis XIV at the apogee of his power and determined to expand France's borders that the Ottoman forces launched a campaign against the Habsburg Empire. Sultan Mehmet IV ruled over the whole of the Balkans and half of Hungary, and was eager for more territory. The Habsburg Emperor Leopold I had focused his attentions firmly on his principal rival, France, and was thus largely unprepared for an attack from the east.

The sultan declared war on 31 March 1683. As the Ottoman troops marched steadily towards Vienna, the city walls (which had been declared 'unsatisfactory' after an official inspection) were frantically patched up. Ammunition and grain poured into the city cellars. Leopold, by all accounts a cautious man and inexperienced in the ways of war, left his capital city to fend for itself. By 14 July the Turkish forces, which numbered at least ninety thousand, had reached the outskirts of Vienna.

Contemporary illustrations give graphic testimony to the starkly uneven contest. In the flat, broad plain of the Danube basin, the city of Vienna huddles behind its thick fortifications. On every side, as far as the eye can see, are the Ottoman Turks and their allies. Close in to the city walls are teams of men digging a network of trenches as intricate as any maze. Smoke hangs in the air as the Turkish cannons regularly discharge their firepower into the city. And further back from the battle front is a vast encampment of tents, soldiers and camels – Istanbul brought to the banks of the Danube.

The siege would last for two months. Despite the carefully devised plans of the city fathers, the starving populace began to eat donkeys and cats. Dysentery and other illnesses were rife. By the beginning of September the situation was desperate.

Leopold I, however, who was installed over 200 kilometres away in the safety of the city of Linz, had not been inactive on his country's behalf, and had recruited an alliance of armies from Austria, Bavaria, Franconia, Saxony and Poland. Individual officers too, from Ireland, England and France volunteered to serve in the ranks of Christendom's armies. Later these soldiers would be instrumental in disseminating the exciting story of the lifting of the siege to their home audiences.

Unusually, it was not the Austrian Emperor who was the commander of the imperial troops but the King of Poland, Jan Sobieski, the most experienced warrior among Europe's monarchs and the most knowledgeable in the ways of the Turk. This was just the kind of contest Sobieski relished, and which he knew would serve to enhance Poland's reputation abroad.

Finally, by the beginning of September, at the same time as the desperate Viennese were lighting their flares from St Stephen's Cathedral, the imperial troops assembled north of the city. Down in the valley, in his sumptuous tent-city with its travelling gardens and harems, the grand vizier was not unduly worried. He certainly did not think it necessary to send reinforcements to his

Iohn the 3.ᵈ King of Poland &ᶜ
the Terror of the Turks

R.Tompſon exc.:

10. 'The Terror of the Turks', one of the many portraits of King Jan Sobieski available after the 1683 Vienna victory.

lightly manned outposts on the two hills in the Vienna Woods closest to the city. This would be his first mistake.

At 2 a.m. on 11 September Sobieski's second-in-command, the refugee French prince Carl of Lorraine, launched an attack on these outposts. Within hours they were in the hands of the Alliance. Now for the first time Lorraine and Sobieski could survey the camp of their enemy: they were terrified by its vastness.[16] For the first time, too, the inhabitants of Vienna could see with their own eyes the troops that had come to their rescue. The premature rejoicing on the city's barricades was loud with the explosions of rockets and cannonfire. Still the Turks did nothing.

At 6 a.m. on 12 September, the Alliance attacked again. It was an attack described by a Turkish observer in terms of awe and wonder: 'they poured down like black tar which destroys and burns everything in its path'. The Turks rallied. Fighting was fierce and the shelling on both sides incessant, a fact confirmed by Sobieski's son Prince Jakub who described in his diary how their breakfast became covered by a thin black layer of ash.

Eleven hours later, sounding the trumpet himself, King Jan Sobieski launched one of the largest military charges in European history. Twenty thousand cavalry galloped down the slopes, jumping over the trenches and breaking through the Turkish artillery. The noise alone must have been impressive: the pounding of horses' hooves, the yells of '*Jesus Maria!*' and '*Bij, zabij!*' ('strike, kill!') and the distinctive sound made by the decorative 'wings' worn by the Polish Hussars – the eerie whistle of millions of eagles' feathers beating the air. Their appearance would have been hardly less imposing. With their richly coloured gowns and fur capes of leopard, tiger and wolf skin, the Poles looked just as exotic as their enemy. Indeed, it was from the Turks (as well as the Tartars and the Persians) that the Poles had been borrowing their fashion sense for over a hundred years. Polish officers informed their troops that the distinguishing feature of the enemy would be their turbans, this being the only item of clothing the Muslim Ottomans and the Catholic Poles were sure *not* to have in common.[17]

Within a few hours, Sobieski had entered the Turkish camp and sent the first news of the victory to his queen. 'This was a calamitous defeat,' wrote the seventeenth-century Ottoman chronicler Silhadar. 'So great that there has never been its like since the first appearance of the Ottoman state.'[18] In Europe, however, it was a victory that was to be savoured, and not only by kings and princes. The wider public was fascinated by accounts of the arduous siege and its dramatic lifting. In the decades following the Battle of Vienna, hundreds of pamphlets and books would be published: anonymous accounts by soldiers who fought in the battle; signed correspondence of officers; and poems, both heroic and satirical. Mass-produced pictures in the form of engravings also spread the word and the triumph even inspired a theatrical production: *Vienna Besieged* opened on the London stage in 1686. After decades of war and hardship, the Battle of Vienna was a story worth commemorating.[19]

As for the Polish king who led the victorious troops, it is no exaggeration to say that after 12 September 1683 Jan Sobieski became a celebrity throughout Europe. Although in German-speaking countries the Poles and their king became famous, or rather infamous, for their allegedly greedy looting of the Turkish treasures, the majority verdict was positive, the printing presses from Italy to Sweden busily churning out likenesses of the moustachioed warrior framed by the words: 'My hand saved, I can truly say, Vienna, Germany and the Empire.' And for those with more homespun tastes, tankards and tablecloths decorated with Sobieski's image were also available.

So pervasive was the fame of the Battle of Vienna, so widespread the renown of its principal combatants, that it is little wonder that the triumph of 1683 is celebrated in local gastronomic folklore. The croissant or *kipfel* is said to have been created when the emperor, grateful for their defence of the city, gave Vienna's bakers the right to make a delicate bread in the shape of the Ottoman crescent. As for the coffeehouses for which Vienna is justly renowned, the Viennese claim that the very first one was established thanks to the discovery of how to make a palatable drink out of the little brown beans left behind by the Turks in 1683.

Nor were these stories confined to Vienna. Immigrant German-speaking bakers who dominated the baking profession in the United States for many years were proud of their ancestors who had played their part in defending Vienna against the Turks, and not just by fighting on the ramparts. Legend has it that a Viennese baker making bread in his cellar bakery foiled an underground invasion of the city when he discovered a Turkish solider tunnelling his way in. To this day the German city of Münster claims this brave baker as one of its own and every year celebrates his contribution to saving Vienna and Europe.

The Siege of Vienna was an event known to all German-speaking bakers in America and therefore one from which many a tall tale could be hung. In time, Jewish immigrant bakers would join the same trade union as the German bakers, the similarities between the German and Yiddish languages creating a particular affinity between the two groups. The legend of a baker commemorating the dramatic victory in Vienna by creating the bagel in the shape of Sobieski's stirrup would have been a worthy counterpart to the legends told about the *kipfel*. It would also have had wide appeal to those immigrants with a link to Polish lands (which so many Jews had) because of the

11. The Münster-born baker foils a Turkish invasion of Vienna.

reputation of Jan Sobieski. It is an attractive proposition; it is also entirely speculative.

Whatever its origin, the story of the bagel being created in honour of Jan Sobieski and his victory in Vienna has endured. Something about it – the disconcerting notion of a Polish king saving Vienna or the strange image of a stirrup serving as inspiration for bread – has continued to capture the imagination. Polish-Jewish historians such as Majer Bałaban who wrote so positively about Jan Sobieski's relations with Jews would no doubt have been pleased (and amused) that a small Jewish roll is keeping Sobieski's name alive for generations of Americans.

CHAPTER 3

RITUALS, RHYMES AND REVOLUTIONS
HOW THE BAGEL LOST ITS
WORTH BUT KEPT ITS VALUE

The first few hundred years of its official existence in Polish lands were trying times for the bagel. The erratic availability of wheat postponed mass popularity, while at the same time the bagel's shape was assuring it a special place in Jewish affections. Economic upheaval and new political movements meant that the bagel was to be found in the middle of the complicated story of Polish–Jewish relations. Both protagonist and bit-player, the bagel provides us with an intimate glimpse of everyday life in Eastern Europe, both Jewish and non-Jewish.

* * *

There was little that was 'everyday' about bagels when they made their first documented appearance. The first mention of the bagel in writing is in 1610 in regulations issued by the Jewish council of Kraków.[1] The council, which oversaw all aspects of communal life, from the naming of the rabbi to maintaining Kashrut (kosher standards) and keeping the streets clean, also took upon itself the

12. A boy pedlar sells bagels in nineteenth-century Poland.

responsibility for limiting the expenditure of individual households. These so-called 'sumptuary laws' were formulated with two
things in mind: to avoid arousing the envy of gentile neighbours
and, in true paternalistic fashion, to make sure that poorer Jews
were not living beyond their means. Only pregnant women, for
example, were to be allowed to wear a ring with diamonds 'because
of [the diamonds'] curative powers'.[2] Otherwise, presumably, such
ostentatious jewellery would be seen as a provocation to passers-
by. Bagels, one assumes, were not as provocative as diamonds, but
they were expensive. With wheat costing four to five times as much
as rye, one can see why the council would have wanted to regulate
their consumption.

Specifically, the bagel regulation in question pertains to the
celebrations to mark the circumcision of a baby boy. In great
detail the document prescribes who may 'send for' bagels, cakes
and challah, and who may receive them. As to the meaning of
these prescriptions, contemporary Yiddish experts do not speak
with one voice. For one they are simply confirmation that it was
common to enjoy different cakes and breads at the celebrations
marking the birth of a boy and his circumcision. Someone else
concludes that the Jewish elders were saying that that bagel is one
of the permitted gifts for a midwife and her attendants following
a successful delivery. In the best-selling book *The Joys of Yiddish*,
Leo Rosten makes a further interpretative leap by asserting that
the 1610 regulations 'stated that bagels would be given as a gift to
any woman in childbirth'.

Whatever interpretation one chooses, what is clear is that
the bagel was sufficiently important as a foodstuff to merit an

appearance in the deliberations of the community, and that it was commonly associated with childbirth. Numerous customs and superstitions surrounded the birth of children and indeed every aspect of life at this time. Circular objects, in particular, were believed to exert powerful protection. The same 1610 regulations refer to the vigil traditionally held by women the night before a circumcision, to protect the child and his mother from the wiles of the demon Lilith, Adam's first wife, who was believed to 'snatch' the newborn. One prophylactic measure commonly taken was to draw a circle around the mother's bed, inside which the names of Adam, Eve and a number of angels for protection were inscribed in chalk. Amulets, often in the shape of a ring with an engraved incantation, were in common use in seventeenth-century Poland. Amulets were also to be found in nature; so-called preserving stones were placed under a pregnant woman's bed to prevent miscarriage, and were of a bagel-like shape: 'pierced through the middle and round about as large and heavy as a medium sized egg [and] glassy in appearance'.[3]

As the golden age of the early 1600s gave way to the calamitous 'deluge' of the mid-seventeenth century, belief in demons and magic became, if anything, more commonplace. The times were uncertain and the Jewish community, in particular, was feeling vulnerable. 'Even if demons had never been created,' observed the Jewish doctor Tobias Kohn in 1707, 'they would have had to have been created for the people of this country [the Polish-Lithuanian Commonwealth]; for there is no land where they are more occupied with demons, talismans, oath formulas, mystical names and dreams.'[4]

It was into this troubled landscape that Israel Ben Eliezer, the man who would become renowned as the Ba'al Shem Tov (known as the Besht) or the Master of the Good Name, was born in around 1700. Ba'al Shems were healers and there were many of them wandering the roads of Poland in those days, offering protection from the evil spirits believed to cause havoc in everyday life. The Besht was one of those miracle men but he was also a charismatic preacher and the founder of one of Judaism's great spiritual movements, Hassidism. He appealed to the ordinary people by preaching a faith which rejoiced in finding God in the natural, everyday world and which valued fervour over scholarship. The love of God was to be celebrated through song and dance and story-telling. It is in one of these stories, popularised and embellished by his disciples to propagate Hassidism to the masses in the nineteenth century that the bagel makes an appearance.

The Ba'al Shem Tov tries to impress on a simpleton the value of a bagel. It is of such worth, he says, that even a non-Jew will help you if you throw him a bagel. A few days later the simpleton falls into a river. As he shouts for help he remembers that he has a bagel in his pocket, fishes out the soggy roll and throws it towards some peasants working in the field nearby. Sure enough, as soon as the bagel lands at their feet they come running and rescue him from drowning.[5] Perhaps promoting belief in the goodness of others, at the very least this story confirms the special affection people had for the bagel. On a less prosaic note, the parable is very much in keeping with the spirit of Hassidism: by sanctifying the mundane, by investing the bagel with significance, the Besht was bringing God closer to his worshippers on earth.

Circular objects, with their intimations of immortality, also figured in rituals associated with death. Bagels became an integral part of Jewish mourning and, indeed, are to this day common fare at funerals. Tisha b'Av, the ninth day of the Hebrew month of Av, is the day on which the Jewish community commemorates the destruction of the Temple in Jerusalem, first by the Babylonians and then by the Romans. On the eve of a day of fasting, it was customary in Eastern European Jewish homes to eat a symbolic meal of 'hard-boiled eggs rolled in ash and each with hard ring-shaped rolls [bagels]'.[6] A nineteenth-century Lithuanian folksong has it thus:

On Tisha b'Av you fast
And it's not right to eat
Before the fast you have bagel with ash
And before you fast you have a full bottle
Until 3 o'clock you recite laments
Afterwards you settle your hungry stomach.[7]

A valued element in religious ceremonies while at the same time part of popular culture, the bagel had entered the canon of Jewish folklore.

*   *   *

Over the course of the eighteenth century, Poland disappeared from the map of Europe. Externally Poland had no clout. Internally every attempt at political reform was resisted by the neighbouring powers of Austria, Prussia and Russia who preferred the country weak and easily manipulated. By 1795, Austria, Prussia and Russia had partitioned Poland–Lithuania into chunks of territory which they proceeded to gobble up. There would, of course, be various episodes of indigestion – uprisings against the tyranny of the foreign occupier – but the overwhelming reality was that until 1918 Poland ceased to exist.

Split into three, the economy of the land that was once Poland suffered. Communication routes which had once been thorough-fares were now subject to international customs' control. The River Vistula, the main conduit for grain, flowed through three countries. Exporting grain was not easy and there were consequently few incentives to modernise what were some of the most inefficient production methods in Europe. Famine was not uncommon for the large majority of people who eked out a living in the country-side, which comprised about 85 per cent of the region's population in the early eighteenth century. Wheat production and consump-tion were low, and people were increasingly relying on the newly introduced potato.

Change was to come in the 1850s. First there was the arrival, by steamship, of American wheat in Europe. This galvanised Russia into exploiting its fertile Ukrainian fields. Modern flour mills were established. At the same time, borders were being opened for trade and the new railways were making transport cheaper. Cheaper wheat meant people began to consume more of it. From 1800 to 1900, the wheat consumption of the average inhabitant of the Russian part of Poland tripled, although, it needs to stressed, in the 1890s he or she was still only eating 57 kilos of wheat a year – or about a kilo a week – compared to 405 kilos of potatoes annually.[8] In other words, a more affordable bagel did not mean that it had become 'everyday' fare in a part of Europe that continued to shock visitors by its poverty.

A folksong of the time illustrates just how little Jewish artisans earned:

> For a tailor to work
> The entire week was his goal
> Yet he earned only a bagel
> With a hole.[9]

More distinguished figures in the community fared (a little) better. Consider this account of how a rabbi in a small town in Russian Poland lived in 1890:

> His salary was 4 rubles a week. A good wage. He used to be a rabbi in a bigger city. There he had the same salary but it was a more expensive place to live so that from one Sabbath to the next they had to live on herring, the staple of the poor. Although for people of their standing the proper diet was: breakfast . . . oatmeal with milk; dinner, half a pound of meat; at night a glass of tea and a day-old bagel.[10]

It is telling that even for 'people of their standing' a 'day-old bagel', not a fresh one, had to suffice.

The irony was that while the Jews often lived in extreme poverty, it was largely thanks to them that the Polish parts of Russia and Austria had any industry or trade at all.[11] Already in the early 1700s, after the collapse of Poland's economy, the towns had been emptying out. Those who could were returning to the countryside where they could make a reliable if minimal living on the land. There were even fears that many towns would disappear altogether. That this did not happen was mainly because the Jewish community had no choice but to stay within the town walls. With the disappearance of the Polish state at the end of the eighteenth century, the dominance of Jewish crafts in urban life increased further. The jobs on noble estates, traditionally held by Jewish administrators, also disappeared as these lands were confiscated as punishment for their owners' participation in anti-tsarist uprisings. The tsar's 1804 decision to keep Jews out of the Russian heartland and confine them to a so-called 'Pale of Settlement' (an area that corresponded more or less to the lands annexed from Poland with the Crimea and Bessarabia added on) made trade with the outside world more difficult. In both the Russian and Austrian parts of Poland, agriculture was dominated by gentiles while the businesses and workshops of small towns were increasingly run by Jews. In many of the smaller towns – or *shtetls* as they are often called – Jews in fact now *were* the majority, their wooden houses and workshops (including bakeries) forming the edges of the central square with the gentiles living on the outskirts.

In general, bakers have a mixed reputation in Jewish folklore. Classified with the working people, or the *proster*, they were also respected because of the central importance of bread. In times of hardship, the Yiddish proverb advises, '*beser dem beker vie dem dokter*': 'better to give to the baker than the doctor'. Some bakers were respected for their wisdom and learning. They knew the laws of Kashrut and more than one story is told of Jewish bakers using the interlude of the dough rising to read the rabbinical commentaries of the Talmud as they smoked their pipes. Others, however, were resented for having too much power and were sometimes suspected of cheating customers by selling underweight loaves.[12]

Bagel bakers did not conform to a single stereotype. On the one hand we are told that bagel making was particularly difficult and dirty work. 'He lies in the ground and bakes bagels' is generally interpreted as meaning that someone is despondent. The exhortation 'go and bake bagels!' was used as a curse not a blessing. On the other hand, the bagel oven is sometimes referred to as the *yiddisher oyvn* or 'Jewish oven' which implies an affectionate relationship between the bagel and its bakers.[13]

The people who made bagels were an eclectic bunch. In the hundreds of 'memorial books'[14] written about the history of the villages, towns and cities of Eastern Europe, we find characters such as Laizer who also played the flute in a klezmer band in a village renowned for its music, and 'tall thin' Shleyme who supported his large family by collecting for the hospital, working for the burial society and baking bagels with 'particularly big holes' for market day. And then there is singing Gdalye, 'the shoemaker who is also a bagel baker'. Gdalye, the Torah reader in the artisans' synagogue, was 'the pride and joy of the workaday Jews'. After baking he went to morning prayers, leaving his wife the task of selling the bagels at market. ' "I'm an artisan, not a salesman," he would argue whenever she put up a fight about having to stand on her feet with the baked goods all day.'[15]

In fact, women both sold and baked bagels: the bagel oven was also known as the *vayberisher oyvn*, or wives' oven. It was an accepted way of making a living for women, as another of the Besht's stories suggests.[16] He tells a young girl planning to convert to Christianity to marry a rich gentile: 'go marry a Jewish baker and sell bagels in the marketplace'. It is unlikely that this was meant as an admonishment as the Besht's philosophy was resolutely not one of punishment, even if someone had considered apostasy. In a community where the highest calling for a man was to devote his life to religious learning, it often fell to wives to work to put food on the table. Women bakers and sellers would have been no strangers to the Besht.

Whoever they were, the number of Jewish bakers in Polish towns and villages rose throughout the nineteenth century, and their customers were not only Jews. The increasingly clear differentiation in economic activity between Jewish and non-Jewish populations brought the two communities together on a regular basis: they were growing ever more dependent on one another. For both gentile peasant and Jewish artisan, the most important day in the calendar was market day, when business was transacted, money was made and conversations took place. This was also the day on which bagels were most in demand.

A nineteenth-century engraving by K. Krzyżanowski shows what must have been a typical market scene. Vendors and shoppers alike are bundled up against the cold, wares transported in sacks slung across the back. A cow awaiting its fate stands patiently on the left while on the right a rather more feisty pig strains at the leash. A pair of boots hangs from a pole resting on the seller's shoulder and in the middle of this mayhem a woman sells bagels from both hands – some strung on a piece of rope, others piled up in a basket.

13. Market day by K. Krzyżanowski.

Easy to carry, easy to eat, the bagel had become the market snack par excellence. Descriptions of market days in the villages and towns of nineteenth-century Eastern Europe always include the sight and sound of the itinerant Jewish sellers – usually young boys and older women – circling the stalls crying 'Bagels! Lemonade! Bagels! Corn on the cob!'[17] As for their customers, many of them would have been non-Jews: the local priest (there was always at least one), as well as the sheriff and the gentile servant girl of one of the better-off Jewish families. Above all there were the peasants who, having spent the night in their wagons in order to sell their vegetables, fowl and firewood first thing in the morning, would have gobbled down a few bagels before spending the rest of their money in Jewish-owned stores on more necessary staples such as salt, shoes and scythes.

Jews and gentiles did not inhabit 'worlds apart': they bought food from one another and ritual foods were exchanged as gifts between friends.[18] Some of the boiled and baked ring-shaped breads sold in the marketplaces of Russian and Austrian Poland were no doubt made by gentile bakers and referred to by them in Polish as *obwarzanki*. But, as Jewish bakers grew in number, this particular bread would increasingly have gone by the name bagel (or in Polish *bajgełe* or *bajgieł*). A dictionary of the Polish language published at the beginning of the twentieth century includes the word *bajgełe* defined – needless to say – as a 'Jewish *obwarzanek*'.[19] The bagel was on its way to acquiring, above all, a Jewish identity in Polish everyday life.[20]

The bagel was a regular fixture not only in the marketplace but also in the adjoining arena of the tavern. As Krzyżanowski's engraving hints, with its queue of people at the door of a rickety house in the square, the tavern did a roaring trade on market day. Another nineteenth-century image reveals the scene behind the tavern door. As a klezmer band plays, a waiter gingerly advances with tray and tankards above his head. In one corner a Jewish child chews on a bagel as he keeps an eye on his goat. Bagels were popular tavern fare. Jewish immigrants to the United States recall parents making bagels to be served at the inn: 'An onion, schnapps and a bagel' would have been a typical order. Too much alcohol led, not infrequently, to drunken peasants smashing up Jewish market stalls. The next market day, however, the same peasants would be pledging allegiance to 'their' Jewish artisans.

14. A nineteenth-century tavern scene. Note the little boy chewing his bagel on the left.

For Jewish artisan and gentile peasant alike, existence was precarious. For adults, the inn provided a rare venue for recreation and relaxation, a place to enjoy a drink and a bagel. For the *shtetl* children, too, the bagel was a treat to be cherished. 'I had no breakfast, only coffee', recalled the great Yiddish writer I. L. Peretz of his childhood in the town of Zamość. 'And following the teachings of the Duties of the Heart I brought my buttered bagel to Avigdor the Teacher's orphaned son who frequented the study house.'[21] It required some discipline, as this anecdote indicates, to forego one's buttered bagel in the morning and do a good deed by giving it to a less fortunate child at school.

Bagel nostalgia is not infrequent in the pages of the memorial books. One woman remembers how as a girl she would wait impatiently for Wednesday to come round, for that was the day Hershel the bagel baker came to town. In another account the excitement at the bagels' arrival and the savouring of their texture and taste are infectious: 'our home became quite merry whenever my *zydeh* [grandfather] Moshe Berz'l came to visit us. He used to come in wintertime. . . . He crossed the threshold with a cheerful *got helf* and . . . he spoke hastily wanting the bagels to arrive warm. His beard and moustache were covered with ice and strewn with fluffy snow and the bagels were indeed still warm, genuine Działoszyc bagels, twisted ones, sprinkled with poppy seed browned to a golden lustre and they crunched gaily between your teeth.'[22]

The ring shape of the bagel, like that of the Italian *ciambella*, provided a host of attractions for children. It was not just that it was easy to eat. It could also be worn as a bracelet, rolled like a hoop and even used to play tug-of-war. 'How many sides has a bagel?' asks one Jewish riddle. 'Two: one inside, one outside.' The bagel was incorporated into all sorts of children's activities. For the younger ones there was the chant to start off a round of blindman's bluff:

Where do you stand? On a barrel.
What do you drink? Apple cider.

What do you bake? Bagels
Catch a bird![23]

For children a little older the bagel played its part in a nonsense
verse to help with learning how to count. Even the rabbi got in on
the act with his ceremonial test for the young boy starting his
formal study of the *Chumash* (Bible). As he stood in his Sabbath
clothes on a table surrounded by proud relatives, the rabbi would
ask:

Enquirer (E): 'Which tome are you studying, young man?'
Me (M):   'The *Chumash*, gratefully.'
E: 'What does *Chumash* mean?'
M: 'Five.'
E: 'Five what? Five bagels for a nickel?'
M: 'No. Five Holy Tomes are contained in the
               Chumash.'

And on it went until the crowd gathered to listen to master and
pupil erupted into a chorus of hearty '*mazel tovs!*'[24]

The author of this particular account was the son of a baker in
eastern Galicia who would, in his own words, become 'the most
skilful bagel-shaper and roll maker' in his father's bakery. Many
years later, after having emigrated to America, he would become
known to the world as a star of the silver screen when he acted
alongside Greta Garbo in *Ninotschka*. Alexander Granach's career
was exceptional. But in his initial impetus to find a better life by
leaving his home town and moving to the big city to seek work,

he was very much part of a mass movement that saw Jews flock to urban centres across Eastern Europe in the second half of the nineteenth century.

* * *

The industrial revolution came late to Eastern Europe but when it did, its cities swelled.

The Jewish community of Warsaw, for example, grew from a mere 10,000 at the beginning of the nineteenth century to over 125,000 strong in the 1880s – at that time the city with the biggest Jewish population in the world. Not far from Warsaw and still in Russian Poland but right on the border with Prussia, the town of Łódź was being developed as Russian Poland's answer to England's Manchester, an East European centre for textile manufacturing. In the early 1800s there were so few Jews there that Jewish baked goods, including bagels, were sold illegally at market. By 1880 Łódź had 580 mills and 45,000 inhabitants. Twenty years later, in 1900, Jewish bakers were numerous and prosperous enough to have built their own synagogue: Łódź had become one of the five largest centres of urban Jewish life in Europe.

Inevitably this rapid urbanisation was accompanied by social dislocation. People were leaving families and traditional occupations behind. In the cities new interest groups were being formed. A Jewish working class was beginning to coalesce politically, uniting around the need to deal with prejudice not only from non-Jewish bosses but also from Jewish ones. In the Jewish middle classes, and especially among the successful new capitalists, assimilation with the Polish language and culture was on the rise. There was growing impatience with the authorities who had traditionally held sway over the Jewish community, and there was fear of and outrage over the political anti-Semitism on the rise across Europe. New leaders were emerging with new ideas.

Two political movements would capture the imagination and commitment of Jews in Eastern Europe at the end of the nineteenth century. Zionism was inspired by the ideas of national unity propagated successfully by European national movements, and Bundism by the ideals of socialism at a time of growing economic and social inequality. Members of both movements were acutely aware that Jews continued to suffer from institutional discrimination and that political anti-Semitism was growing in strength. Founded officially in the same year, 1897, they had very different messages to deliver. One advocated the creation of a Jewish state in Palestine while the other staked its claim to a socialist homeland in Eastern Europe by vowing to achieve equal rights for the Jewish worker. What they shared was a commitment to creating a Jewish political framework within which Jews could decide their own fate.

Bakeries played a key role in spreading the news of political change. The memorial books tell of earnest but discreet debates between Zionists and Bundists as activists from both camps spread out to recruit supporters while seeking to evade the police who in Russia were constantly on the look-out for anything challenging tsarist authority. Bakeries provided a perfect cover and were often the main social gathering place for the village or townsfolk. They were also places where young women could go alone without giving their parents cause for concern. Many a young woman was thus engaged in socialist conversation while she waited at the bakery on the Sabbath to pick up her mother's *cholent* (a ready-prepared stew of beans, barley and meat which had been cooking in the baker's oven). The crowd of young people that gathered of an evening outside the baker's shop for their bagels was also a rich

15. The Selling bakery in Eastern Galicia at the turn of the century.

recruiting ground as the activists expounded their arguments in village after village, town after town.

The Bund had its origins in the revolutionary idealism of urban Russian-speaking Jews, young intellectuals who wanted to see the autocratic tsar overthrown. Initially, they had little in common with the mass of their co-religionists, the artisans and workers who spoke Yiddish and lived in small and medium-sized towns across the Pale of Settlement. Also, once these intellectuals embraced the cause of the specifically Jewish worker they had a massive challenge on their hands. By working to awaken class consciousness, they were dividing the traditionally united Jewish community, turning Jewish worker against Jewish boss at a time when anti-Jewish discrimination was mounting. Nevertheless, their message of better working conditions and shorter working hours was a powerful one.

Bertha Fox was one of the young people attracted to the Bund and its ideology. Writing in an autobiographical essay many years later,[25] she recalled how the secret lectures in the woods and clandestine meetings in the shoemaker's cellar equipped her with the knowledge and self-confidence to demand better conditions at work and to quit when her demands were refused. Bertha's next job, at a tobacco store, was, she writes, better because it had set hours, good pay and 'tea and bagels'.

Bakers themselves, particularly those employed in the bigger bakeries of large towns, were prime candidates for Bund membership. Bakery workers endured notoriously difficult working conditions and toiled for long hours at night for little pay. The memorial books tell a number of stories about bakers joining the Bund, some of whom became firebrand orators for the cause. Bakers' strikes were not infrequent. In one case a fight broke out between those bakers (mostly single) who wanted a strike and those (mostly with a family) who did not. Tempers became frayed and shots were fired inside a bakery, killing one of the owners. Despite all this agitation, these particular bakers in the town of Bobruisk did achieve their aim of a twelve-hour day and a later start time on Saturday (midnight), albeit with a proportionate dock in pay. But there were also the unlucky bakers who got arrested by the police and exiled to Siberia. Still others, having escaped detention, joined the hundreds of thousands of Jews leaving for America and a new life.

At its height in the early 1900s, the Bund could claim 30,000 members,[26] some of whom were as young as ten. Its success, despite being an illegal organisation in tsarist Russia and its commitment to the Yiddish language, contributed significantly to the growing confidence of a secular Yiddish culture. This confidence, in turn, would have an impact on the image of the bagel.

* * *

Until the nineteenth century Yiddish, the language spoken by Jewish communities across Eastern Europe, had been thought of in a somewhat dismissive fashion as an argot, a 'kitchen tongue' spoken by women and the working people and used to refer to mundane objects such as the bagel. In contrast, Hebrew was the language of scholarship and high culture. But in the second half of the nineteenth century, serious Jewish writers began to eschew Hebrew as well as Polish, Russian and German in favour of Yiddish.

Yiddish folklore became their inspiration and the richness of the Yiddish language their seducer. 'I fell in love with Yiddish,' wrote Mendele, the founder of modern Yiddish literature, 'and wedded her forever.' It was a love affair that would be joined by thousands of practitioners and, consequently, revelled in by millions of readers who could read *only* in Yiddish. I. L. Peretz, the writer who gave up his buttered bagel as a child, would become known as another of the masters of literary Yiddish. Peretz began to write in Yiddish only at the age of forty, having already been recognised as an accomplished Hebrew poet. He was to become not only a wildly popular author – his funeral in Warsaw was attended by a hundred thousand mourners – but also a champion of Yiddish, the language in which, as he said, 'we [the Jewish people] will gather together our treasures, create our culture, stimulate our soul, and unite ourselves over time and space'.[27]

The cultural élan experienced at the beginning of the twentieth century by the proponents of Yiddish literature and culture was reflected in how they wrote about bagels. It was not just that the bagel, as a staple Jewish food and a favourite in folklore, was a regular presence in stories and poems; it was also that the perception of the bagel's essence changed. Now the focus of the story-teller and poet was not so much on the substantive ring of dough – whose ingredients, as we have seen, were increasingly common – but rather on the infinitely expandable bagel hole.

The inspiration for according special status to the bagel hole may well have come from a group of characters with their own special status in Jewish folklore: the sages, or fools, of Chelm (Chełm), 'the *ne plus ultra* in simpletons' who, as one folklorist quips, 'find the most intricate ways of doing the most stupid things'.[28] Finding Chelm's bagels lacking, a delegation of the town's sages decide they must act and find out why the neighbouring town's bagels are tastier, crunchier and chewier. 'It's simple,' says the neighbouring town's bagel baker when they ask him, 'it's the hole that makes the bagel.' 'Please,' beg the delegation from Chelm, 'can we have some of your holes so as to improve our bagels?' 'Of course,' answers the baker and hands over a dozen or so holes which the sages place very carefully in their pockets. Wending their way home in high spirits, they stop paying attention to the path. Suddenly all of them – to a sage – fall over the crest of a hill and roll down, the bagel holes falling out of their pockets as they gather speed. Desperately they search the fields for these special holes, but to no avail. Crestfallen they return to Chelm empty-handed, unable to change the sorry state of the town's bagels.

We can laugh at the naïveté of the gentlemen from Chelm, so easily hoodwinked and so delighted with their bagel holes. But while these gentlemen may be a little lacking in sophistication they are also supposed to be learned, the humour in the tales about them often coming from the tension between their bookishness and their wide-eyed unwordliness. For them the bagel is not any old bread: it is a special bread – a bread at whose centre is a hole. But what does that hole represent? Nothingness? Infinity? What a feast for intellectual discussion in a small roll. As the material value of the bagel was shrinking and life was generally becoming harder, Jewish culture found humour in the infinite flights of fancy to which the bagel's shape could give rise.

The Romanian-Jewish poet Eliezer Shtaynbarg was one of the modern practitioners of Yiddish literature who celebrated the bagel and its hole. The nub of his fable 'The Bagel Hole and Two Brass Buttons' is what happens to the bagel hole once the 'rope of dough around it' has been eaten and the hole has been put in Shloyme's pocket alongside two brass buttons. The buttons – 'rabble rousers' according to the poet – are insulted to be in a pocket alongside a bagel hole:

> Who should they latch on to? What is their goal?
> For after all, what's a bagel hole?
> One big naught! Let's mock it!

The hole, however, fights back:

> Lo, behold, the bagel hole answers freshly – you ought to be
>   ashamed.
> Materialists! You lack all sense. Your brain is maimed.
> Do you think the bagel's more important than its essence?
> Are you running from the spiritual idea? Its presence
> Is indeed the central core and cause of every entity,
> Even of crude brass
> So rude and crass
> Just out of curiosity
> Cut the brass in pieces and then with care
> Slice the smallest sliver thin as hair
> Then slowly further subdivide it like one divides the year
> To months and days, hours, minutes, seconds. Isn't it quite clear

That now you're at the bagel hole, the rounded zero?
Do you grasp the thesis? Think! Now you have a mere 0.
Its profundity assess and cogitate![29]

'Its profundity assess and cogitate!' It is a poem the fools of Chelm would have approved of. For all its ubiquity at the market-place, the inn and the railway station at the dawn of the twentieth century, the bagel was still special, its place and its value in the affections of Jewish consumers assured.

CHAPTER 4

BAGEL POLEMICS IN AN INDEPENDENT POLAND

> I think we can say of Jewish history in interwar Poland that
> it was 'the best of times and the worst of times'.
>
> Ezra Mendelsohn[1]

Like all the states newly created out of the collapse of the Austro-Hungarian Empire, Prussia and Russia in 1918, Poland was faced with a veritable mountain of problems. Somehow it had to rise from the rubble of three empires. At the same time, a recently constituted Polish army rallied to defend its new capital Warsaw – and arguably Western Europe – from Soviet aggression. The chaotic situation was further complicated by the growing tension between the proposed model of a nation–state and the fact that Poland was one of the most ethnically heterogeneous countries in Europe. Almost a third of the population was ethnically non-Polish, 10 per cent of the total being Yiddish-speaking Jews.[2]

Many in the Jewish community were apprehensive of, and in some cases opposed to, the new state and its leaders' calls for 'national unity'. There were, however, others who held out great hopes for what an independent and democratic Poland might offer. For all the hostility towards ethnic minorities that existed in Poland, there were undoubted gains to be made for the Jewish community in the new situation. By the beginning of the 1920s Jewish political parties had been created and Jewish deputies elected to the *Sejm* or Parliament. Jewish charities and schools were being established. Jewish trade unions had begun to operate in the open. Independent Poland could legitimately lay claim to having more Jewish organisations than any other European country.

The short life of the Second Republic, snuffed out before its twenty-first birthday by the Nazi invasion, was a tumultuous one. It was, however, in this brief period of upheaval, between 1918 and 1939, that the bagel would come of age politically.

Produced principally by Jewish bakers and sold mainly by Jewish pedlars, the bagel was a snack available on almost every street corner in almost every town in Poland, consumed and enjoyed by people of every ethnicity and class. The bagel was a Jewish product that was an integral part of Polish everyday life. As such the bagel and the plight of its pedlars was enlisted by artists and writers (not all of them Jewish) in their arguments for a better society, especially as the economic situation became desperate and anti-Semitism more virulent. Paradoxically, the bagel's increasing visibility was testimony to the dynamism of Polish Jewish culture in this period. These were, indeed, both the worst and the best of times for Jews in Poland.

* * *

It is a small picture (Figure 16 on p. 72) – one of six scenes of
Jewish artisans and craftsmen painted with jewel-cutting
precision. A sweating baker, his broad shoulders bare under his
white overalls, his knees bent and muscular arms taut, is shovel-
ling out of the oven a pair of plump challahs. To his left his
co-worker bends over a rectangular trough, presumably checking
the rising dough. And to his right, next to a couple more challahs
and a squat loaf of rye, are eight golden bagels.

The picture is from a modern illumination of the Statute
of Kalisz by the Polish Jewish artist Artur Szyk. Alongside beautiful calligraphic translations of the obligations and privileges
accorded to the Jews in 1264 by Prince Bolesław the Pious, Szyk
paints the story of the Jews' contribution to Polish life – from the
building of cities in the fourteenth century and the shipping of
grain to the rest of Europe in the sixteenth, to the Jewish heroes
who spilt their blood in the cause of Polish independence in the
nineteenth and twentieth centuries. From the extraordinary to
the ordinary. One of the plates extols the crucial contribution
Jewish artisans made to the economic health of Poland across
the centuries: on a page proudly embossed with the Polish
eagle and a sword-wielding knight on horseback are the tailor,
the cobbler, the weaver, the watchmaker, the blacksmith and the
baker.

The baker and his bagels made this cameo appearance in
the years 1928 to 1933, touring fourteen Polish cities as well as
appearing at much talked-about exhibition openings in Paris
(where Szyk had studied), Warsaw and London. The artistic reviews

16. The industrious baker in Artur Szyk's illumination of the Statute of Kalisz.

were enthusiastic. As for the message Szyk sought to promote – Poland's history of tolerance and the integral part played by Jews in Polish life – there were certainly a number of individuals in Polish public life in the 1920s who wanted to promote it too. At a time when the country's treatment of its minorities was being scrutinised by the international community, what could be a better calling card than Szyk's *Statute of Kalisz*? As the Polish Ambassador to London remarked to the *Jewish Chronicle*'s correspondent at the gallery opening there: '[this is] the work of a great Polish artist who is at the same time a Jew. The motives of [sic] all his paintings were not motives of an ordinary kind but of a very high idealism.'[3]

Inside Poland, too, the timing of Szyk's painting was significant. The country's government had just been overthrown in a *coup d'état*. The man who led the coup, Józef Piłsudski, had been instrumental in creating independent Poland eight years earlier. Born in Lithuania, Piłsudski's vision of the Polish nation was a broad one, based not on blood but on shared history and culture. He was not a proponent of 'Polonising' the country's ethnic minorities. 'Poland,' Piłsudski is said to have quipped, 'is like an *obwarzanek* [bagel]. The best bits are on the edges.' Whether or not Piłsudski was thinking of the *obwarzanek* as Jewish, he was intimating his attachment to the ethnically mixed borderlands of the new state. By dedicating his *Statute of Kalisz* to Józef Piłsudski, Artur Szyk was not just expressing his admiration for Piłsudski and his love for Poland, but was also making an appeal for a fairer, more tolerant future.

In 1931 Szyk would receive the Gold Cross of Merit from the Polish government for his service to the nation through art. Not all in Polish officialdom, however, were happy with the recognition

17. Jozef Piłsudski is greeted by a delegation of Jews after the Polish Army liberated their town from the Bolsheviks in 1920.

accorded him. Petty bureaucrats complained that there should be 'no place for Jews in the artistic life of Poland'. Presumably, they found it difficult to accept that Szyk's portrait of the baker (and the tailor, weaver, cobbler, et al.) extolled an economic reality clearly visible for all to see in independent Poland: the vital role played by Jewish artisans.

The importance of Jewish artisans to Polish economic life had only grown since the nineteenth century. Ironically, increased hostility towards the Jews coincided with an outpouring of Jewish scholarship about all aspects of communal life, including its economic activities. Economist Ignacy Bornstein was one of those scholars. His 1936 survey (in Polish) *Jewish Crafts in Poland* was lauded by its publishers as a 'pioneering work . . . given the paucity of material on the subject . . . and the separateness of the Jewish community'.[4] According to Bornstein, bakers were the third largest group of Jewish artisans in Poland after tailors and tanners. In the mid 1930s, he estimated that 48 per cent of all the country's bakers were Jewish: in some cities in the east of Poland the figure was as high as 70 per cent. The Jewish community may have been separate, but its presence was keenly felt, not least on the household bread run.

Of the Jewish bakers of Kraków, one family dominated: the Beigels. Their family name makes one sit up. Legend has it that one Shlomo Beigel baked bagels in Frankfurt and at some point in the 1800s moved his family and business to Kraków. Not an explanation accepted by all, it is, however, true that eighteenth- and nineteenth-century Austrian bureaucrats were keen to systematise their Jewish subjects and were not averse to assigning professions as surnames. If Cukierman (from the German word for sugar, *zucker*), Singer and Goldschmidt came about in this way, why not Beigel? It certainly did no harm for a business to have the same surname as one of the products on sale. According to the Beigel descendants,[5] there were at least six bakeries belonging to the extended family scattered around the city. The daughters of bakers Fischl Beigel and

Abraham Grienberg (a Beigel son-in-law) recall with nostalgia the 'wonderful smell of the bakery' kept 'immaculate' with daily washing of windows ('I have never seen such cleanliness in the US or Israel'), the 'big bagel kettles in the kitchen', the 'very special English oven – not Polish – as big as a room!', the 'crispiness' of the bagels and the 'pride' at seeing boxes with their name on them being filled with rolls and tied shut with coloured ribbons.

These were Hassidic families whose daughters went to Polish state schools, learned the romantic Polish poets by heart (which they can still recite in their eighties) and spoke Polish with their siblings at home. In the afternoons they had private religious instruction. The Grienbergs ran the bakery together, rising at 5 a.m. to count out the wholesale goods which were distributed every morning by wagon. Mother manned the counter during the day and Father oversaw the work of the Jewish and non-Jewish helpers. In the afternoon, after drawing up the bills, Mother would take a nap and Father would go to pray at the synagogue around the corner. Life was not easy: new dresses came only at Passover and Yom Kippur.

'Backward' is a word often used to describe the Poland that reassembled itself in 1918. The economy was overwhelmingly agrarian and little had changed since the nineteenth century: Polish agricultural yields, for example, were a quarter that of Germany. The Wall Street Crash of 1929 proved a decisive body blow. Prices collapsed, peasant incomes evaporated and with them tax revenues. Journalists, both foreign and Polish, reported seeing people in the Polish countryside cut matches into four parts in order to save money. Potatoes were boiled in the same water day after day in order to save salt. Poland was indeed, as one of its prime ministers bluntly put it, 'a land of paupers'. The life of the small-town Jewish artisan may have been a bit easier than that of the peasant in these times, but only just. There was no money to buy meat or sugar or bread and so bakers in the Warsaw region saw demand for their produce slump by 30 per cent in 1934.

18. Bagels being sold in the snow in rural Poland, 1938.

The deprivation in the big cities was catastrophic. In Warsaw, for example, it is estimated that 80 per cent of Jews were living in poverty, many of them kept alive only thanks to the work of Jewish charities. Official anti-Jewish discrimination made the situation even more difficult. Government credits were rarely extended to Jewish businesses, and businesses that had survived the 1929 crisis were also less likely to employ Jewish workers, who were perceived as more militant (even when the factory owner was Jewish). None of these difficulties, however, protected the Jewish community from being objects of envy and resentment. With the death of Józef Piłsudski and the deepening economic crisis, the calls from nationalists to 'Polonise' the economy became louder. Individual activists called for a boycott of Jewish shops. Young thugs attacked Jews in the street: in 1936 there were over six hundred such attacks, including thirteen murders.

The government reacted equivocally. In a speech to parliament the then prime minister, Felicjan Sławoj-Składkowski, warned that 'all anti-Jewish excesses without exception are being and will be severely punished', but went on to call for more business competition 'whatever one's name and one's origin'. 'One should not resort to violence,' he said in what would become the most infamous sentence in the speech, 'but an economic fight – by all means!'

At the same time, the government was introducing various policies to regulate the work of all artisans. On the surface they seem reasonable but in practice they were to prove debilitating to many Jewish bakers. New licensing laws, for example, were designed to create common standards across the industry, but the written exams were in Polish which put many Yiddish-speaking Jewish bakers at a distinct disadvantage. Sunday was promulgated by parliament as a day of rest in keeping with the Catholic week, but Jewish bakeries were already shut for religious reasons on the Jewish Sabbath, Saturday. Most onerous financially was the government's drive for bakeries to introduce mechanical ovens, which were modern, clean and very expensive. Most Jewish bakeries were small family businesses with only a few helpers working alongside the owner. This requirement finished a number of them off altogether. At the well-established bagel businesses in Kraków the women remember 'a lot of taxes and a lot of inspections'. There was, however, some elasticity in the system: the elder sister remembers going herself to the tax authorities to persuade them to charge the now struggling bakery less than it was initially assessed for. She also remembers bribes being given to hygiene inspectors: 'They were always trying to catch us out. If we gave them money then it was OK. They knew the Jewish people would pay bribes.' None of the women remember any nationalist boycotting of their fathers' bakeries – on the contrary they talk of a number of loyal gentile customers, including their Polish school teachers.

The Beigels and Grienbergs were relatively better off than many Polish citizens. The sisters remember with especial pity the poor people (mostly Jewish) who would come in to the shop with a basket or long pole to buy a few dozen bagels to hawk in the street. In small towns bagel peddling may have been a respectable way to earn a living but in the big city it was, it seems, an occupation of last resort.

* * *

As many economists pointed out at the time, the dramatic increase in street trading in Polish cities was a very bad sign. The writer and parliamentary deputy Ignacy Schiper observed: 'you need only look at the groups of pedlars selling chocolates, shoelaces and bagels which now swarm the streets of almost every town in Poland to understand to what an alarming extent [Jewish] trade has been impoverished.'[6] In 1934 Rafal Mahler, a historian and Marxist, was commissioned by *Economic Life,* one of the many new Yiddish-language scholarly journals being published in Poland, to investigate the bagel pedlars of Warsaw.[7] Why bagels and not peas or Seltzer water or chocolates? Mahler does not say, but it could well be because the bagel's plight, given its special cultural pedigree, resonated in a particularly poignant way. Whatever the reason, his detailed study, based on questionnaires handed out to 129 members of Warsaw's Bagel Sellers' Union, provides an intimate glimpse into the lives of these itinerant sellers. They were mostly men but there were also some women, who tended to be older, often widows, since young girls would not be out on the streets 'for obvious reasons'. Of the estimated six hundred bagel sellers in Warsaw, only thirty were Christian. Over a third of the men were young boys, although the ranks of the adult male pedlars were growing as unemployment in other crafts increased. Most of these men had once been tailors or shoemakers; some had been bakers. Two thirds of the pedlars interviewed had come into the business only since the economic crisis of 1929. The fact that these men had turned to bagel peddling was, observes Mahler, a concrete indication of a society breaking down.

19. A family of bagel pedlars in Warsaw.

Pedlars took bagels on commission from bakeries comprised of circles of bakers who clubbed together to rent premises from other larger bakeries. These premises were generally in cellars, and in the memoirs of the baker and unionist Bernard Goldshteyn,[8] made the other bakeries in Warsaw look like 'palaces' in comparison. The basket was generally provided by the bakery. Pedlars would hawk their wares (which were notorious for going stale quickly) to strollers in the park and late-night theatregoers, regularly working until 1 a.m. On average, pedlars had to sell to at least forty-three customers before making 1 zloty profit. They rarely made more than 2 zlotys a day, the equivalent of what the average factory worker then made in two hours.[9]

Peddling was illegal without a state permit. Since this was an expense most pedlars could not afford, they spent much of their time worrying about being caught, having their bagels confiscated and passing up to three days in jail. Unionist Bernard Goldshteyn describes how the pedlars dealt with the 'enemy' or the police. When they worked as a group they operated a 'security system' whereby one of their number acted as look-out. If he (or she) gave a sign that a policeman was coming, the person with the basket (often a young boy since he was the fastest), would run off to hide. Passers-by would also help out by shouting a warning – 'Run!' or 'Six, six!' There was, recalls Goldshteyn, the occasional decent policeman who, when no one was looking, would themselves tell the boy pedlars to run.

This precarious existence – more than half shared a room with at least five others and almost half shared a bed with more than two people – could be too much for some. Mahler describes a former bootmaker, a husband and a father, who sells 200 bagels every evening but has already tried to commit suicide once and continues to contemplate doing so because he is so afraid of being arrested. Another man, a former shoemaker, has already spent forty-eight hours in prison and, because he can't find the money for the fine, has been unable to return home to his family for four months. A twenty-one-year-old mother works until 1 a.m. every day because her husband, a former baker who once did the peddling, is in jail (probably for peddling without a permit). The most unusual case Mahler records is that of a single young woman of twenty who managed to escape an inquisitive policeman by running away, but in so doing fell under a tram and lost her leg. When Mahler interviewed her she was continuing to sell bagels, hobbling along on her wooden prosthesis.

For all his professionally neutral tone, the images summoned up in Mahler's survey are filled with pathos and drama. The desperate nature of these people's lives was on display every day in cities across Poland. It is, therefore, not surprising that in these same years poets such as the Kraków songwriter Mordechai Gebirtig would devote not one but two of his songs to the plight of the bagel pedlars. In one a woman pedlar is arrested for not having a licence. In the other, '*Di Mame*' (The Mother), a daughter sings a lament for her mother and for her own life:

Soon the Sabbath starts, Mama told me not to fight in the yard.
Mama stands a whole day in the street selling bagels.
See to it, Leah, she said, that the baby should not be wet
And Motel should go to school, not run around here and there.
. . . .
Soon the Sabbath starts, Mama is not here yet
Perhaps the policeman arrested her on the street?
Just a week before, hopefully not again, he confiscated
The basket with bagels. Had to pay a fine as well.
I open the window all the way

I cry and I look down at the yard.
All the windows are lit up, except ours, alas.
Yosele and Berale
Chavale and Perale
Are singing songs, are happy and I envy them.[10]

Non-Jewish observers, too, began to equate bagel peddling with grinding poverty. The socialist activist and writer Wanda Wasilewska was one of the loudest voices raised in protest against anti-Jewish politics in interwar Poland. 'Why look for those responsible for Poland's economic problems elsewhere,' wrote Wasilewska, 'when it is so easy to find them nearby, in a street of the Jewish quarter? . . . when it is so easy and so safe to vent one's anger in a fight with a bowed porter, with a Jewish boy selling watches, with an old Jewish woman selling bagels.'[11]

In 1934, the same year as Mahler's study, a rallying cry in defence of bagel pedlars was published in the pages of *Wiadomości Literackie* (*Literary News*), one of the most influential Polish-language publications of the period, beloved of both the Jewish and non-Jewish intelligentsia and one of the few journals to challenge the growing anti-Semitism of the late 1930s on a regular basis. 'Many city courtrooms,' the article begins, 'make their living, quite simply, off *obwarzanki* [bagels]. These cases, a dark stain on society's conscience, are at the same time the quintessence of a particular social hypocrisy.'[12]

The author of these fighting words was Irena Krzywicka. The daughter of assimilated Polish Jews whose socialist leanings earned them Siberian exile, Krzywicka broke many taboos in independent

Poland, writing (among other things) about homosexuality, female sexual desire and contraception. She believed in trying to make people change their perspective – about bagel sellers too, evidently. Krzywicka describes a few of the 'transgressors' as they testify in court. 'The old lady had no age and no face. She was shaking with fear, her eyes darting around.' The policeman testifies that he arrested her because she was selling from a dirty basket. The woman responds: 'Mr Judge, how am I to know if it is a clean basket? I wash it every day and a new one would cost 2 zlotys. If I sell all my *obwarzanki* I will only make 50 grosze. My husband doesn't work and I have three children.' The judge's verdict: a 10-zloty fine. 'But where will I get 10 zlotys?' 'If you can't find it,' counters the judge, 'then you'll go to jail.' In another case the seller defends herself: 'Yes, the basket was on the ground, but I am sick and just wanted a rest. I am a widow with six children. What am I to do? They have nothing to eat.' The judge's verdict this time: a 5-zloty fine. 'But my children, they will die of hunger! The eldest is only 8 years old!' And the judge's response? 'I can't help it.' The article concludes with a passionate plea for basic social justice made by someone who has observed at close quarters the plight of the bagel pedlar:

In this current intense crisis when unemployment is raging and poverty more monstrous than an epidemic of the plague, sticking to narrow-minded hygiene regulations . . . is inhuman cruelty. Cooked peas in a dirty cloth may not be healthy but is starving healthy? Is living with 12 people in a room healthy? Is it not time that society put some food in their cupboard[?]

Irena Krzywicka was appealing to Poland's intellectual elite to change government policy towards street pedlars. For all its righteous passion and Krzywicka's not inconsiderable standing in certain social circles, there is no evidence that her article had any impact whatsoever. For Jewish activists trying to alleviate the poverty of their co-religionists, the message was clear: they had to do it themselves.

One of the organisations to provide concrete assistance was the General Jewish Workers' Alliance, the Bund. The Bund had had a shaky start when it first emerged from the political underground into an independent Poland. But over time it established itself as a political party to be reckoned with, as an effective organiser of trade unions and as an important educator. For the starving children of the crowded inner cities the Bund offered unimagined respite: a modern sanatorium in the countryside just outside Warsaw. In 1935 the Bund commissioned a film – an early docudrama – to promote the work of the sanatorium and raise money for it in Poland and overseas. Much hope was pinned on the emotional impact the film would have. Bagels and their pedlars were cast in a crucial role.

Mir Kommen On (*Here We Come*) begins, as the narrator puts it, 'in the miserable slums, byways of doom where the sun throws shadows instead of warmth and light'. The tenement buildings are grimy, the streets crowded, children emerge from their cellar homes to peddle on the pavement. The camera zooms in to focus on a group of scruffy-looking boys holding large baskets of bagels. Suddenly, over the cacophony of street calls and the unsettling notes of violins, a whistling is heard. The children dash into a dark back alley to escape. But as they run, most of the bagels spill out of the baskets and with them the children's income for the day. The camera closes in and lingers for a few seconds on the bagels as they lie on the ground. The narrator intones: 'Once again they flee, even denied the right to earn their daily bread.' Later in the film some of these same boys come to the sanatorium and are

20. The caption in a 1927 edition of the *Jewish Daily Forward* in New York reads: 'This cute vender of bagel [sic] . . . is looking out for the police because he does not have a pedlar's license as required by Warsaw law.'

transformed: by sunshine, socialist solidarity and regular meals – with baskets of rolls and bagels clearly visible on the canteen tables.

An uplifting story on film as well as in life (the sanatorium treated over ten thousand children in its fourteen years of existence), *Mir Kommen On* did not find favour with the Polish government censors who deemed it to be 'feeding off the misery of the masses and promoting a communist message'. They demanded that a number of scenes, including the one with the unfortunate bagel pedlars, be cut. The director refused and the film was banned, never to be officially shown in interwar Poland. It was, however, screened privately, receiving enthusiastic reviews in the Yiddish press and the influential *Wiadomości Literackie*. In Paris it was introduced at the prestigious Salle Pleyel by the young Luis Buñuel. In New York it proved, as had been hoped, an effective fundraiser. Such was the paradox of interwar Poland. On the one hand, official government figures submitted to the League of Nations stated that six million Polish citizens were on the verge of starvation; on the other, government censors objected to a scene showing the desperation of life on the street. On the one hand, the 1930s witnessed a rising tide of official and semi-official anti-Jewish discrimination; on the other, Warsaw was said to set the cultural tone for the Yiddish-speaking world.

Despite the dire economic situation and the worsening ethnic tensions, the cultural scene – both non-Jewish and Jewish – in Poland's capital city during the 1920s and 1930s can only be described as effervescent. For the first time in over a century Poland was a free country, a country in which people could, on the whole, say what they liked. After so many decades of repression, this freedom was a tonic, made all the more intoxicating by the possibilities for popular culture presented by the arrival of radio and cinema.

Within the Jewish community creative energy was further enhanced by the existence of three different but overlapping Jewish cultures – in Hebrew, Yiddish and Polish. In Warsaw alone there were fifty separate publications in Yiddish. Writers residing in Poland regularly contributed to the Yiddish press in New York, while Yiddish-speaking actors from the United States regularly came to Poland to make films for worldwide Jewish audiences. Jewish writers, artists and actors were playing leading roles in Polish culture. The editor-in-chief of *Wiadomości Literackie* was Jewish. The man whom consensus has crowned the twentieth century's greatest Polish poet, Julian Tuwim, was Jewish. And if assimilated Jews such as Tuwim were in a minority, there were nevertheless many middle-class Jews who spoke Polish and enjoyed Polish culture, while at the same time speaking Yiddish. Inevitably, Yiddishisms – such as the word *bajgiel* instead of *obwarzanek* – were creeping into everyday Polish usage, as Polish-language dictionaries of the time confirm.

One place where Yiddish was almost obligatory in Polish culture was at the cabaret. Warsaw's cabaret scene was boisterous and very fashionable. Frequented by the moneyed classes, the city's cabarets provided an attractive mix of hit tunes, political satire, literary wit and the odd bit of nudity. Every revue had to have a few *szmoncesy*, a word whose literal meaning in Yiddish is 'nonsense' or 'trifle', but which came to mean 'Jewish quip or comical sketch' in Polish. As one Pole recalled many years later: 'part of the *bon ton* of the day was to know all the Yiddish jokes, the *szmoncesy* of comedians . . . and to weave them into conversation'.[13]

Andrzej Włast was one of the most prolific writers for the cabaret and produced hit after hit. As the artistic director of one of Warsaw's top nightspots, Morskie Oko, he followed the trends in Paris and Berlin, always on the lookout for numbers he could adapt for his audiences. One evening he put a singing bagel pedlar on stage. It was to prove a hit.

The song had originated in Odessa in 1926 during a period of political thaw in the Soviet Union and used the private enterprise of selling bagels – in Russian *bublitchki* – to poke fun at the nonsensical aspects of soviet life.[14] Within a few years, *bublitchki* had been banned by the authorities in Moscow. But its catchy tune, adopted from a klezmer staple, and the popularity of its Russian lyricist meant that it was quickly picked up by both the Yiddish and Polish-language revues. Its political bite was lost in both translations; the song pulls instead at the heartstrings of its audience, especially since on their way home they were bound to pass a pedlar with a basket of bagels.

> The dead of night draws near
> The wind blows in the lantern
> Who does not listen to my song?
> Only perhaps the devil.
> I wander where fate chases me
> Even though half the town knows me
> And no one even looks at me
> Nor at my stall.

Oh buy my *bublitchki*
Fresh bagels
When you give me *rublitchki*
I will feed you.
I only have one wish
Before the stars go out
Remember poor me
At least one time!

The Yiddish version is even more affecting:

With little strength I walk these streets
Evicted and unwanted everywhere
My clothes are torn I am unwashed
With tortured thoughts I wander about

Buy bagels
Fresh bagels
Buy quickly please
I need to sell
For I am poor and lost
And homeless in this world.

*   *   *

As it turned out, these last two verses were to prove chillingly
prophetic for the Jews of Poland. On 1 September 1939 the Nazis
invaded from the west. Jewish soldiers – one hundred and fifty
thousand of them – were part of the courageous defence effort,

which was all too quickly defeated. On 17 September the Red Army invaded from the east. Poland had once again ceased to exist, severed by two of the most murderous regimes in European history. In German-occupied Poland steps were soon taken to segregate the Jews from the rest of the population; in Warsaw a third of the city's inhabitants was forcibly resettled into 2 per cent of the city's land. At its peak, over four hundred thousand Jews, many of them sent in from outside the capital, would reside in these 375 acres. A little over a year after their invasion, the Nazis cut off all contact between these people and the rest of the city: from November 1940 the Warsaw ghetto was 'closed'.

In the dire circumstances of Nazi-occupied Poland, asking what happened to the bagel seems a frivolous question. But more than one ghetto diarist writes of bagel sellers. Epidemiologist Ludwik Hirszfeld noticed them on his first day in the Warsaw ghetto:

[It was] a crowded stinking prison where we ceased to be human beings. . . . The people looked like ragamuffins; they were in rags, even without shirts. Hundreds of them, mainly women and children, were selling various things right on the streets: buttons; thread; old clothes; pretzels; cigarettes; some exotic sweets – anything. The street had a music of its own: an indescribable hubbub and buzz in which one could discern the thin resigned voices of children: 'Bagels, bagels for sale, cigarettes, candy.' It was impossible to forget those weak children's voices.[15]

Where had those bagels come from? In 1941 when Hirszfeld wrote the above diary entry there were still functioning bakeries in the Warsaw ghetto, their official task being to make enough bread to fulfil the rations allotted to each Jewish inhabitant, but unofficially they baked other blackmarket goods with flour smuggled in from the Aryan side. People were desperate to make money in any way they could in the nightmare they were now living. All but the very rich smugglers were constantly hungry. It was not just that paying jobs were hard to come by. It was also a fact that there was very little food available inside the ghetto walls. The Nazis made sure that the Jewish daily calorific intake was less than one-tenth of theirs – and six times as expensive. In an obscenely distorted echo of the 1610 Kraków regulation concerning bagels, in the Warsaw ghetto there was a German-run, Jewish-manned network which was supposed to prevent, among other things, the production of luxury goods such as white flour rolls.[16]

It was not long before bread had to be made with any vaguely appropriate ingredient one could lay one's hands on. 'The bread is dark,' wrote another Warsaw ghetto diarist, 'and tastes like sawdust.'[17] Dark bagels, too, would soon make their appearance, their sad sales pitch immortalised after the war by the Vilnius poet and partisan Sh. Kaczerginsky:

My father and mother and brother Zamele
My little Nechamela are all no more.
My only little girl in her only frock
Stands here and sells small *beigelech*

Buy ghetto *beigelech*, small as honey cakes
Only a mark a *beigele*

Made of black dough
Buy it from my little girl.

As for the people who made and sold bagels, the overwhelming majority – the bakers and pedlars – would die in the Holocaust. After running one of the sanctioned bakeries (and an illegal soup kitchen) in the Kraków ghetto, the Beigel family were deported to the Płaszów concentration camp: only two daughters and a son would survive. The songwriter Mordechai Gebirtig was shot in the Kraków ghetto in 1942. Cabaret lyricist Andrzej Włast, born Gustaw Baumritter, worked in the most popular of the Warsaw ghetto's café-cabarets. He too would be shot dead by the Gestapo as he tried to pass through one of the ghetto's gates to hide on the Aryan side. Journalist Irena Krzywicka spent the war in hiding, under an assumed name. In 1945 she moved to France. Bagel surveyor Rafal Mahler was one of the few who emigrated to America in the late 1930s. He would then go to Israel where he became a professor at the University of Tel Aviv. Artur Szyk also went to the United States where he became well known as an anti-fascist artist, his cartoons reportedly more popular than the pin-ups of Hollywood starlets. His fame led Hitler himself to order the death of Szyk's mother, Eugenia, and it was to her that Szyk dedicated one of the first books he illustrated after the war.

In March 1943 my beloved 70-year-old mother Eugenia Szyk was taken from the ghetto of Łódz to the Nazi furnaces at Majdanek. With her voluntarily went her faithful servant, the good Christian, Jozefa, a Polish peasant. Together, hand in hand, they were burned alive. In memory of the two noble martyrs I dedicate my pictures of the Bible as an eternal Kaddish for these great souls.[18]

CHAPTER 5

BOILING OVER
THE IMMIGRANT BAGEL AND THE
STRUGGLE FOR WORKERS' RIGHTS

It is impossible to say for certain when the bagel made its first appearance on American soil. What is clear is that the bagel – or, more accurately, the new immigrants' steadfast craving for it – played a role in the subsequent development of the Jewish labour movement in America. New York's Jewish bakers' dreadful plight would galvanise the public and politicians. Their struggle to achieve decent working conditions would be joined by a wide section of the city's Jewish community, not least by ordinary housewives encouraged to buy only union-made bread and bagels. It was on the Lower East Side of Manhattan Island, at the turn of the nineteenth century and into the twentieth, that the bakers' union movement reached boiling point. Their achievements would be such that by 1910 the Jewish bakery unions of New York City were being held up as role models to bakers across America.

*   *   *

The year 1882 saw the beginning of a mass exodus of Jews – men, women and children – from Eastern Europe to America. Over two million people arrived in the years leading up to the First World War, an annual average of more than sixty thousand. Carrying little more than small bundles of clothing and about $26 worth of savings, the majority headed straight for the crowded streets of the Lower East Side of Manhattan Island. The bucolic idyll summoned up by street names such as Cherry and Orchard may have struck many of the newcomers, themselves so often from small towns and villages, as surreal. What the new immigrants found was a brick, iron and tar jungle of narrow streets clogged with pushcarts, shoppers and mounds of garbage, while the huge protruding 'zeds' of fire escapes and the profusion of shop signs made the buildings seem even closer to one another than they actually were. The sky was hardly to be seen from the street. Even breathing was difficult. 'The pent-in sultry atmosphere,' wrote the journalist Abraham Cahan, who himself had arrived in 1882 from Russia, 'was laden with nausea and pierced with a discordant and, as it were, plaintive buzz. Supper had been despatched in a hurry and the teeming population of the cyclopic tenement houses were out in full force "for fresh air" as even these people will say in mental quotation marks.'[1]

Most of the greenhorns fresh off the boat were employed in the sweat shops of the garment industry. The invention of the sewing machine and the development of 'section work' – 'the most ingenious and effective engine of over-exertion known to modern industry' – meant that anyone could now make a coat or a pair of slacks. Men who had been honoured as scholars in the Old

Country found themselves working in stifling, cramped tenement rooms next to former water carriers and single young women. In 1880, 28 per cent of New York's workforce were employed in clothing manufacture. By 1910 that figure had almost doubled, to 46 per cent.[2]

The burgeoning Jewish community needed kosher food and hence the religious supervision of baking to guarantee there had been no contact with forbidden fats or meats. Food provided one of the few available constants and comforts in these new alien surroundings. 'Like every foreign colony in this city,' Abraham Cahan observed, 'the Russian and Polish Jews cling to their methods and form in the matter [of bread].' The new immigrants wanted bread which tasted the way it did back home: dark rye loaves, braided challah and, of course, bagels.[3]

To begin with, the bagel continued to serve the ritual purpose it had in the Old Country. 'Tomorrow is the ninth of Av,' noted Cahan in a piece he wrote for English-language readers in the summer of 1898:

the anniversary of the fall of Jerusalem and the destruction of the Temple by Titus. ... It was after 12 o'clock when a stout woman in a great black wig came into the bookstore of Mr Katzenelenbogen, Canal Street, near Allen. She carried a huge paper bag of bagels (ring shaped cakes), eggs and a pitcher of milk. 'Give me two knoths (elegies) and a Book of Lamentations; hurry up, mister, do me a favour. I have left the baby alone,' she said anxiously, as she waddled up to the counter.[4]

Bagels were soon part of everyday life in New York. Indeed, in America bagels were cheaper than in Europe. An 1891 guidebook for would-be Jewish immigrants from Russia assured those 'who aspire to bread and pickles in America' that they could earn 50 cents a day, spend 10 cents for coffee and bagels and save 40 cents. But the cheap bagel came at a human cost.

Bagels were part of the standard selection produced by bakeries on the Lower East Side whose numbers increased as the immigrants flooded in, totalling seventy shops by 1900.[5] Bakeries were relatively inexpensive businesses to start up in those days: all one needed was space and an oven, or at most $200. There was no need to acquire much machinery (and what little of it was required was available) since the workforce was so easy to come by – and so easy to replace should the workers not be able to survive the conditions.

The conditions were terrible. The Lower East Side bakeries were located mainly along or, to be more precise, *under* Hester and Rivington Streets, down steep flights of stairs to a space rarely higher than 7 foot. Because of the rudimentary ovens, the temperature was fierce and, on the whole, impossible to control. There was no ventilation. Bakers worked stripped to their waist for thirteen or fourteen hours a day, seven days a week. Typically young and unmarried, they often lived at their workplace sleeping between the mounds of rising dough and the oven with cats, rats and cockroaches 'as big as birds' for company. Illness was common and lifespan short. And if they did somehow manage to find a wife and start a family, it was not unheard of for bakers not to recognise their own children, so rarely were they at home.

21. Most early Lower East Side bakeries were located in the cellars under Hester Street.

Hyam Plumka was seventeen when he arrived in the United States and began working as a bread carrier.[6] The son of a wealthy fur trader fallen on hard times, Plumka certainly did not find the 'streets of gold' he had expected in America as he worked on Hester Street in the 1890s. 'Such slavery went on in all the bakeries. . . . The workday was eighteen hours in a twenty-four hour period – from four in the morning until ten at night. . . . On

Thursday nights the bakers did not let me sleep at all.' His description of how bakeries cut corners turns the stomach:

> In every Jewish bakery the bakery bosses used 'spoiled eggs', that is, eggs that were already very old and could not be sold. The bread carrier had to gather them and put them in a big cup. When I went to gather the eggs, it didn't go well. For inside some of the broken eggs were 'little animals'. Some of the eggs gave a little burst when I cracked them open. My hands became full of white worms. The worms were crawling all over the shells of the eggs. . . . Every baker used the spoiled eggs. . . . The same kind of cheating went on in all the Jewish bakeries.

Bread carriers like Plumka were at the bottom of the bakery's hierarchy, but as he himself observed the life of the skilled bakery workers was not much better.[7] When the bakery worker did eventually venture out into the light of day during those few hours between mixing the dough and its proofing, it was usually to the local saloon to have a beer and play cards. But this free time was far from free. Saloons like Rosner's on the corner of Ludlow and Hester Streets also served as employment agencies. The baker who had been 'given' a job by someone within a particular saloon was expected to return exclusively to this establishment to consume his beer and play his game of cards. It was known as the 'vampire system'.[8]

Other obligations also constrained the new immigrant workers. Many of their bosses were *Landsleit* – coming from the same town or village in Europe – to whom a letter of introduction had been provided by a neighbour or a neighbour's neighbour. Work relations

22. Hyam Plumka – by then a *former* bakery helper – in the 1920s.

were therefore a tricky business. Clubs and associations organised around the members' home towns (called *Landsmanshaftn*) were the mainstays of social life on the Lower East Side, and loyalties to the Old Country initially trumped any sense of workers' solidarity; it was hard to complain about working conditions to a man seen back home as a benefactor.

Despite the miserable working conditions and the cruel disappointment many must have felt, the new arrivals were not, to begin with, interested in challenging the system. Exhaustion was an obvious but not insignificant factor. At the same time, there was little desire to limit working hours; every extra dollar earned meant a dollar saved for a wife's or parent's Atlantic passage. Every dollar gained also meant a step closer, if the worker so desired – and many of them did – to becoming the boss. All this meant that the Jewish labour movement in the United States, including bakers, would get off to a slow start in the 1880s. The first specifically Jewish bakers' union, Local 31, was formed on the Lower East Side in 1885 but soon fell apart, and two separate attempts to resurrect it failed. Brief, enthusiastic strikes were followed by the bosses reneging on their promises, disillusion among the workers and long periods of union inactivity. It would take a group of other workers to organise the bakers into something more lasting.[9]

* * *

'Pale-faced, hollow-chested, listless, and brutified, they [the bakery workers] seemed to be hopeless material for organisation and struggle.'[10] Morris Hillquit, the author of this bleak judgement, was an immigrant from Latvia and one of a group of young Jewish intellectuals who spent the hot summer evenings on New York's tenement rooftops discussing how to change the world, if not the working lives of Jewish immigrants:

> Here was a situation that fairly cried out for sympathy and help. Our group was quick to heed the summons. We resolved to undertake the task of bettering the lives of our laboring countrymen, of educating them to a realisation of their human rights, of organising them for resistance to their exploiters and of securing for them tolerable conditions of labor and life.

In 1888, Hillquit's group formed the United Hebrew Trades (UHT), with the express aim of building a 'Jewish labor movement . . . from the top down'.

Their socialist message fell on fertile ground. Uprooted from family and tradition, struggling to make ends meet in an alien environment, this newly formed working class was hungry for social justice and inspiration. People flocked to lectures about the principles of socialism. Standing room only meetings between groups of workers and the UHT representatives were held in synagogues. Who was Moses, asked one worker organiser newly won over to the cause, if not the Jews' first union walking delegate?

The members of the Journeymen Bakers' National Union, established a few years earlier in 1886, were similarly wooed. The UHT leadership was keen to work within the wider American labour movement. The response of the Journeymen Bakers' Union was immediate and positive. Dominated by German bakers, it was eager to show its internationalist credentials. At the same time, its members felt a particular solidarity with these Jewish bakers who spoke a 'German dialect' and – crucially – were not about to take their jobs since they baked primarily for Jewish customers. Last, but certainly not least, the economy was booming. And so in 1890, the Jewish bakers' union banner was retrieved from the pawn shop and the Jewish bakers' Local 31 was again open for business.

The National Union's official paper, the *Bakers' Journal*, wrote in enthusiastic terms of the 'remarkable example . . . given by the Hebrew trades . . . lifted up to self-confidence and manly resistance!' It urged its readers to overcome any prejudice they might have:

> It was left to our stalwart Jewish . . . comrades to give an example of union spirit and courage. . . . The very men whom you are pleased to look upon with contemptuous smiles . . . give an example of manhood which radiantly shines forth in their love of liberty and self assertion.[11]

Local 31's membership grew slowly but gradually. By 1891, it was the third largest union in what was now called the Journeymen Bakers' and Confectioners' International,[12] with widespread public support on the Lower East Side. The union label, a small square or circle of paper pasted on to the crust of baked goods to show that they were made by union members, had proved an effective and popular tool. The socialist Yiddish-language *New York People's*

23. The *Bakers' Journal* was the paper of the Journeymen Bakers' National Union.

Journal urged its readers to 'buy no bread [other] than that which carries the union label'. Jewish bakers needed 200,000 labels a week to satisfy demand and the *Bakers' Journal* reported that 'the Jewish working population has become so much accustomed to the label that it is a very powerful weapon for the union'.[13] Indeed, so powerful a weapon had it become that some bakery bosses actually resorted to producing counterfeit labels to attract custom.

By 1893, however, Local 31 would cease to exist. With the economy entering a depression, 100,000 people found themselves unemployed in New York City alone. The situation on the Lower

East Side was exacerbated by the continuing arrival of large numbers of immigrants, willing to work at any price. These were not circumstances conducive to union solidarity: bad conditions of work were better than no work. But for the bakers of Local 31 the problems were also ideological. Local 31 was the child of two rather different parents with clashing political aspirations: the radical UHT and the more conservative Bakery Workers' International. The International, a founding member of the American Federation of Labor (AFL), was more interested in working within the capitalist system to achieve benefits for its members than fighting for socialism. In stark contrast the UHT saw capitalism as 'an unjust system which must be overturned' and in its place must be built a truly humane society. Increasing tension between the UHT and the International forced Local 31 to choose sides. Having initially stuck with the International, the Jewish bakers saw their support in Jewish Manhattan melt away. Unable to provide comparable popular backing, the International indignantly withdrew from the fray, henceforth vowing that there would be 'no extra charters to Jewish bakers'. For the next fifteen years, from 1893 to 1908, the Jewish bakers of the Lower East Side remained outside the mainstream American labour movement. But this did not mean that they and their supporters were inactive.

* * *

One year after the demise of Local 31, Bernard Weinstein, secretary of the United Hebrew Trades, was sitting in his office when he was called out to an emergency. A baker had collapsed while working in the middle of the night and was now terribly ill. 'It was with great difficulty,' Weinstein wrote, 'that we were able to get into the "mine" which was called a bakery . . . two or three small men, half naked were kneading the dough, one poured out his heart to us as we stood by the oven. The filth everywhere was terrible . . . When we came back to [the] office of UHT we had a meeting. The result was that two days later I went to [the] factory inspectors and I told them what I saw in the bakery. They decided to set up an investigation of all bakeries on [the] East Side – Jewish and non-Jewish.'[14]

Weinstein's protest came at a propitious moment. Earlier that year a series of newspaper articles had once again drawn the New York public's – and, crucially, the politicians' – attention to the miserable living conditions of the city's poor. At the same time boards of health across the country, in Chicago and San Francisco as well as in Brooklyn, were looking into the health ramifications of dirty bakeries. Medical studies had confirmed that a loaf of bread could easily transmit contagious diseases.

If previously New Yorkers had been happily eating their bread and bagels without a thought about where they were made, they were soon to be shocked into awareness by a report headlined 'Bread and Filth Cooked Together', which appeared in the *New York Press* in the autumn of 1894:

Trays of pretzel biscuit [that is, bagels] more or less fresh from the oven, stood upon the barrels. . . . The wooden floor was rotten and bent under the weight of a person in every part . . . and wet, so wet that if a man stepped on that portion the splash of the water underneath could plainly [be heard]. . . .

The shop was thoroughly infested with a great variety of insect life . . . real genuine cockroaches, about an inch long, were seen springing at a lively rate in the direction of the half moulded dough.[15]

Edward Marshall, the author of this article and editor of the Sunday *New York Press*, was already known for his advocacy of policies to alleviate the poverty so rampant in Lower Manhattan. Whether Marshall and Weinstein were aware of each other's work or not, both interventions, together with a campaign by the International, helped create enough of a public consensus to get a Bakeshop law passed unanimously in the New York State Assembly in the spring of 1895.

The new law banned employees from sleeping in the bakeries; specified the drainage, plumbing and maintenance necessary to keep the bakeries sanitary (cats were specifically allowed to stay on the premises – presumably to deal with the rats); limited the daily and weekly maximum of hours worked; and established an inspectorate to make sure these conditions were met. The legislation was soon replicated in other states of the Union. For the first time, standards had been established in writing, codified in law and backed with a bureaucracy charged with upholding these standards.

That is not to say that victory was complete. The number of inspectors was small and too often the bureaucrats turned a blind eye to problems in order to meet their targets. The state, in other words, did not have the means to enforce compliance across the board. It was up to the bakery workers to remain vigilant. The irony, of course, was that sustained vigilance was not feasible without a union.

Something even more ironic occurred when an upstate New York baker, Joseph Lochner, attacked the Bakeshop law. Lochner, who had been convicted of forcing his employees to work longer than sixty hours a week, appealed to the Supreme Court in 1904. His argument was that limiting the hours a baker works was a violation of the liberty of contract, and therefore made the Bakeshop law a violation of the Fourteenth Amendment of the Constitution and its clause 'nor shall any state deprive any person of life, liberty or property without due process of law'. The majority of justices agreed. 'There is no reasonable ground,' Justice Peckham's decision reads, 'for interfering with the liberty of person or the right of free contract by determining the hours of labor in the occupation of a baker.... There is no contention that bakers as a class are not equal in intelligence and capacity to men in other trades and occupations, or that they are not able to assert their rights and care for themselves without the protecting arm of the state.' As Justice Oliver Wendell Holmes recognised in his dissent, the Lochner decision had a significance far beyond the working hours of bakers. Through this ruling the Court had very much aligned the Constitution with a set of pro-employer, laissez-faire principles which, as Holmes commented, 'a large part of the country does not entertain'. It was an alignment that would cast a long shadow over American law, society and politics until the late 1930s, a period which would come to be known as the 'Lochner era'.[16]

In the bakeries of the Lower East Side the reaction to the verdict was disbelief. 'I have often wondered,' wrote bakers' champion

Morris Hillquit, 'whether Mr Justice Peckham and his four concurring associates would have felt quite so certain about the capacity of the bakers to assert their rights and to exercise "their independence of judgement and action" if they had . . . accompanied Bernard Weinstein in his mission of help to the sovereign and independent baker who fell in the midst of his free labour like an overburdened beast.' As for the bakers themselves, thanks to the Lochner decision their working conditions swiftly and significantly deteriorated. Unsurprisingly, their frustration boiled over. Led by an inexperienced young firebrand by the name of Samuel Kurtz, they went on strike in August 1905. Things soon turned violent. Kerosene was poured on dough and set alight; delicatessens selling non-union bread were attacked; loaves being delivered from union bakeries outside the city were destroyed. Not all the violence was caused by strikers, but public sympathy began to fall away. After a month the strike collapsed, having achieved worse than nothing. The bakeries of the Lower East Side were now full of non-union men and around five hundred union bakers without jobs were fanning out across the Eastern seaboard looking for work.

The situation seemed calamitous. In fact, things were soon to look up.

The one steadfast supporter of the bakery workers' strike of 1905, and indeed of the bakers' struggle for many years, had been the social democratic *Forward* newspaper. The *Jewish Daily Forward* was more than the most popular Yiddish-language newspaper in America; for its readers, it was teacher, friend and mentor. Its editor, Abraham Cahan, was one of the co-founders of the United Hebrew Trades alongside young fellow idealists Morris Hillquit and Bernard Weinstein. Cahan was determined to use the newspaper to engage the average Jewish immigrant in America. His early radicalism had undergone a softening: capitalism would have to be tamed rather than overthrown. Unionism was the answer, not revolution. Cahan was also a believer in community responsibility and in what solidarity among Jewish workers in Manhattan could achieve. 'It is wholly a domestic matter with us,' he wrote in an editorial commenting on a yet another bakers' strike:

> The workmen are ours and the bosses are ours, and we alone are the customers. . . . Let us show the world that when a struggle like this occurs in our midst, we settle the question in a feeling of justice and human sympathy – that we settle the issue in favour of the workmen and their just demands.

With Cahan at the helm, it was inevitable that *Forward* readers would become more sympathetic towards the bakers. At the same time, the Bakery and Confectionery Workers' International, barely coping with the chaos up and down the Eastern Seaboard caused by out-of-work bakers from New York City, decided the time had come to deal with 'the New York problem'. Jacob Goldstein from Boston was sent to 'try to bring order amongst the New York Jewish locals'. Note the use of the verb 'try'.

Jacob Goldstein, 'strong, of athletic build with bushy hair, a heart of gold and a convincing voice', was the organiser of Local 45 of the Bakery Workers' International in Boston. A native of Riga,

24. Pioneering newspaper editor Abraham Cahan.

he had started out as a garment worker but in 1904 threw in his lot with the bakers after witnessing a particularly brutal instance of death by exhaustion in a Boston bakery. AG, a Polish-Jewish immigrant baker, writes enthusiastically of Goldstein's first appearance in New York at the International's 1905 convention:

> There then appeared a certain Jacob Goldstein, a representative of the Boston Jewish Bakers' Union. He himself wasn't even a baker. With strong arguments he demonstrated that Jewish bakery workers could definitely be organised, just like workers of other nationalities, and perhaps even better, if only we would try to organise them. And Goldstein's speech had such an effect that the convention designated money to organise the East Side Jewish bakers. And the International borrowed this same Goldstein from the Jewish Bakers' Union and made him the special organiser for New York. Goldstein had a silver tongue and a golden heart. He knew how to touch the heart of each listener, especially the bakers. . . . How can I describe the way Mr Goldstein just started speaking and immediately found his way into our hearts? That we just started following him, like children follow their mother.[17]

It was, however, far from plain sailing in New York for Goldstein, despite his silver tongue. By the end of 1906 he had managed to amalgamate three Jewish locals into one but he still faced challenges – a not insignificant problem being a two-year economic down turn, always a difficult time for unions and a boon for left-wing radicals with an anti-capitalist agenda. These tensions were being played out on the Lower East Side as they were across the country. But by late autumn 1908 the bakers of the Lower East Side had rejoined the International – after an absence of fifteen years – in the newly chartered Local 100. The stage was now set for the strike that would usher in one of the most important years in Jewish labour history.

*   *   *

The 1909 strike began, as most strikes had previously, at the beginning of May. The bakers were demanding a maximum ten-hour day; a minimum salary; recognition of the union and use of the union label. They also added to their list something for which the Jewish labour movement was to become famous: that the bosses allow their workers to give one night's work to unemployed bakers:

> The Jewish locals demand from their steady men to support the loafing men, not with money but with work. . . . [We] take the list of loafing men and the list of steady men and [determine] just how much the steady men must give up of their time to enable the loafing men to get enough work to cover their immediate expenses and a little above.[18]

The baker bosses refused to countenance any of these demands. They had high hopes that this strike would be a repeat of the 1905 disaster where violence alienated the public and reinforced the open shop. It was indeed a bloody strike. 'Bricks Fly Thick in Bakers' Fight,' ran the *New York Times* headline; 'Strikers Storm East Side Shops – One Raider's Skull Fractured with Sugar Bowl'.

But this time, most of the reporting expressed scepticism as to how much of the violence was being caused by the strikers and how much by the bosses.

Furthermore, this time the International supported the strike. Money was collected for a strike fund; plans were drawn up for a cooperative bakery and crucially Jacob Goldstone (he had changed his name from Goldstein in 1907) came down from Boston to run the union during the strike. Realising how vital community support would be, he made sure that the housewives of the Lower East Side were able to buy union bread from the Bronx and Brooklyn. The price housewives were paying for community solidarity was high: 18 cents for a loaf which would normally have cost 8 cents. But people were willing to pay it.

On the day following the first delivery of union loaves a special conference entitled 'The Bakers' Strike Must Be Won' was launched by the union, the *Forward* and a number of other organisations. The express aim of the three-day meeting was to rally the local community to the cause. It was a resounding success. 'That strike,' Bernard Weinstein commented later, 'stirred up the whole Jewish community.' Money poured in to support the striking bakers. Civic organisations such as the Women's Trade Union League provided more than support: they publicised the cause through their own investigation into the 'horrible conditions in which bakers are forced to work' which, as the *Bakers' Journal* observed, 'will certainly create a sensation among bread consumers'. As the strike entered its fifth week there were no signs of it breaking, although the effort did nearly break Jacob Goldstone's health: he had to retire to Boston to recover.

Finally, in the seventh week of the strike the Hebrew Master Bakers of the Lower East Side capitulated. Recognition of the union, a closed shop, higher wages – all were achieved. 'The victory,' wrote Abraham Cahan, 'belongs to the entire Jewish quarter – to the many thousands who have refused to eat scab bread and who have given the strikers moral and practical support.' Charles Iffland, the International's representative who had taken over from the exhausted Jacob Goldstone, paid homage to the New York public and went on metaphorically to shake the white overalls of the other – non-Jewish – bakers in the city:

> Don't be afraid, come out from behind the bush and try to help those who help all year by contributing to the organisation so as to keep up the wages in our trade and conditions in reasonable hours. Are you not ashamed [*sic* – he must have meant to include 'in front of'] of your brothers who have fought and won better conditions than you have? Make good and show them that we are willing to stand shoulder to shoulder. Never mind what race we are.[19]

On the afternoon of 2 July a parade of people five thousand strong marched through the streets of the Lower East Side. At the head of the procession was an enormous loaf of bread, over 15 feet long and 5 feet wide.

Having been the object of the International's ire fifteen years earlier, the Jewish bakers had now established themselves as model unionists. They would continue to hold that enviable position for some years to come. In 1910, Local 100 could count 1,500

25. On 2 July 1909 the triumphant bakers marched through the Lower East Side of Manhattan carrying a loaf of bread five feet wide and fifteen feet long.

members on its books who in a further show of confidence and pride had organised themselves into autonomous sections according to their special skills – including one for bagel bakers. That same year the Jewish bakers of New York won a nine-hour day – without a strike. The following year they refused to negotiate with any associa-tion of master bakers instead insisting on dealing with the bosses on a bakery-by-bakery basis. They were turning the tables on the employers and winning. The Treasurer of the International, A. A. Myrup, stated categorically in his 1911 report on the 'situation in

New York' that 'only the Jewish organisations are really active and they are doing wonderful work for the organisation'.[20]

The 1909 bakers' victory was also a turning point for the entire labour movement on the Lower East Side. Their achievement ushered in a period during which the Jewish labour movement as a whole came to play a leading role among American unions, most famously in the garment industry with the resurgence of the International Ladies' Garment Workers' Union (ILGWU). The 1909 bread parade was proof positive to the labour activists in the garment industry that better conditions were attainable. Eventually, the community solidarity on the Lower East Side which had served the bakers so well would do the same for the much greater numbers of seamstresses, pressers, tailors, knee-pants and shirtwaist makers.

Frank F. Rosenblatt of the Bureau of Philanthropic Research was emphatic, if a little defensive, in his written assessment of how things had changed in the 1917 *Jewish Communal Register of New York*:

> Prior to 1910 . . . the Jew as a trade unionist, as one of a well-disciplined bona-fide organization, as a mere dues-paying member, was considered almost an impossibility, because of the strong individualistic peculiarities which were attributed to him. . . . The new environment in this country has greatly changed the peculiar 'psychology' of the Jew. The Jewish worker is now recognized not only as an excellent striker but also as a first-class union man, loyal to his organisation and devoted to its interest.

CHAPTER 6

'KINGS OF THE LINE'
THE STORY OF BAGEL BAKERS
UNION LOCAL NO. 338

In March 1950 the editors of the *Bakers' and Confectioners' Journal* ran a cover feature on the art of bagel baking. Working on the correct assumption that this 'exclusively Jewish bread product' would have been unfamiliar to most of their readers – members of the Bakery and Confectionery Workers' International Union (B & C) – writer was elaborate in his description:

> Walking into a bagel bakery gives you the feeling that you are entering another century. The air is thick with the flavour of the Old World, because modernism has no place in an establishment which produces this ancient Jewish bread product. . . . Bagel baking has been a Jewish art for centuries and today men of the Bakery and Confectionery Workers' International Union turn out bagels which would be a credit to their ancestors.

The bagel was an anomaly: a bread that was holding its own against the 1950s' trend towards increasingly homogeneous food, the product of a baking process that remained resolutely old fashioned and unmechanised:

> One of the first things that strikes you when you enter is the simplicity of operations. This is due largely to the absence of streamlined equipment, which is scorned by the bagel artist. While your sense of smell is captured by the mellow, sweetish scent of the expertly blended dough, your ears pick up the rhythmic thump-thump, clap-clap of the men who are cutting and twisting the mixture to form the doughnut-like bagel. They work with the precision of highly trained athletes. Operating in teams of two, the twisters exercise a sense of timing and caution against lost motion which would make the most skilled boxer moan with envy.

It is rare for the prose of the *Bakers' and Confectioners' Journal* to reach such heights of lyricism, but the bakers of bagels were a rare breed among their fellow unionists. With no machines to undercut them, they could name their price. They were paid 'by the piece' (the number they turned out) but, as the *Journal* explained, 'don't be misled by the sparse-sounding phrase. The fact is that these men are among the highest paid in the baking industry, some of them earning more than $150 a week.' With the median weekly wage in New York City then standing at $56, there is little doubt that the bagel bakers of Local 338 were indeed 'the kings of the line'.

The 1950s would see the high point in the union's fortunes, an extraordinary time when it was impossible to sell a bagel in New York City without their say-so. The story of Local 338 is in many

26. The *Bakers' and Confectioners' Journal* received an award for this cover in March 1950 for its '"texture" photo of bagels . . . a favourite Jewish bread shaped like a doughnut.'

ways the fulfilment of the promise that America offered to those immigrants looking for their streets of gold. But success on this scale bred a dangerous complacency. It is a sad irony that Local 338 folded just as the bagel was beginning to seduce mainstream America.

* * *

Seducing the public at the beginning of the twentieth century was the industrially made white loaf. Even in the Jewish community, as the influence of the immigrant generation waned, consumers started to look elsewhere for their bread. The author of a 1928 article in the *Jewish Bakers' Voice* entitled 'A True Story', was shocked to be served white sliced bread at Sunday dinner in a Jewish household:

> I would rather not have eaten it with my meal but I was a guest in another man's house and I thought it best to say nothing. I took a slice of the bread, bit into it and found it to be exactly what I had expected. No taste, no delicacy, no satisfaction for the palate, a poor quality of straw. . . . Finally I lost my patience and burst out to the mistress of the house, 'You will excuse me. Your cooking is so wonderful . . . and yet you eat this bread. It is straw, it has no taste, I can't keep it in my mouth, it is no bread for a man, but a fake. . . . What surprises me is that I should find this kind of stuff in a Jewish home. The Jew knows very well what the Jewish baker makes, he has been brought up on the Jewish baker's bread and I do not see how he can turn away from it in favour of something like this.[1]

27. An advertisement from 1929 in the *Jewish Bakers' Voice*.

But turn away he did. By the late 1920s it was estimated that 60 per cent of the bread consumed in Jewish neighbourhoods was white and 'non-Jewish'. Rye bread, thought to be too central to the Jewish cultural identity ever to be replaced, was being eclipsed. 'One may actually cover the whole city', the *Jewish Bakers' Voice* observed with sadness, 'and never find any display of rye breads.'[2]

Jewish tastes in America were becoming Jewish American tastes, the shift in bread-eating habits a modest but concrete indication of the cultural assimilation that was taking place.

The Jewish demand for bagels, on the other hand, was steady – if restricted to the weekend. The bagel seemed to exert an emotional pull for more than a few American Jews, people who had left their immigrant parents and their Yiddish ways behind on the Lower East Side, but who nevertheless did not want to sever cultural links with their past completely. Bagels – easily obtained and identifiably Jewish – had established themselves as a family Sunday breakfast tradition.[3] It hardly seems a coincidence that a 1951 theatre revue, whose audiences one critic described as 'a culturally hybrid variety of American Jew', was entitled *Bagels and Yox*.[4] The majority of reviewers sneered – just as later observers would sneeringly dismiss suburban 'bagel and lox' Jewishness – but the 'hybrid' audiences kept on coming.

One of the attractions of *Bagels and Yox* was the fact that freshly baked bagels with cream cheese were handed out to the audience during the interval. For the month of December 1951 and the beginning of 1952, however, the audience had to make do with doughnuts. Once again Local 338, the bagel bakers' union, was on strike.

∗ ∗ ∗

The strike of 1951 was a very different affair from the chaotic protests earlier in the century. It was peaceful, it was disciplined and the outcome – a victory for the union – was predictable.

While the bagel bakers had come a long way since the establishment of their first autonomous section in 1910, their power,

28. The title of *Bagels and Yox*, wrote one bemused reviewer, 'refers to bagels, hard rolls which, for some unknown reason, have acquired a comical connotation among comedians.'

ironically, derived from the fact that the process of bagel baking had not progressed at all. Bagel bakeries were still housed in cellars, ovens were still coal-burning and bagels were still hand rolled. Rolling the bagels was the most skilled work in the bakery and arguably the most demanding. The average output for a roller in Local 338 was between 700 and 830 bagels an hour, or one bagel every 4 to 5 seconds, and on a weekend shift the roller was expected to keep this up for ten hours on his feet. There was no machine capable of doing this work. Inventors had tried, but all attempts ended in the bagel's tough dough getting the better of the bit of metal. From 1937, the year it became a fully fledged independently chartered union, Local 338 controlled the supply of a handcraft which seemed impervious to any mechanical challenge – a fact its members exploited to their advantage. Strikes were common: union leaders did not hesitate to withdraw their labour if they felt their interests were threatened, even in wartime. The bakery owners, represented by the Bagel Bakers' Association, were in a decidedly weak position.

The 1950s was a good decade for organised labour in America but even against this generally positive backdrop the bagel bakers' Local 338 was special. They had maintained what amounted to a closed shop, they earned some of the highest wages in the business and they enjoyed excellent benefits – not just pension and health plans but dental and eyeglass insurance too. Of particular significance was the fact that their contract was annual – a rare arrangement at a time when most bakers' unions settled for three-year contracts, and advantageous given that the employers were so dependent on their employees' skills.

29. A member of Local 338 stringing bagels for distribution to retail bakeries and delicatessens.

There was, of course, a downside to working in such a resolutely old-fashioned industry. To begin with there were the sanitary – or, rather, unsanitary – conditions. The cellars were dirty, often with no running water or bathroom facilities. Bagel bakeries were so filthy, reminisces one baker, that it was not unusual for workers to change into their work clothes in the street, even in winter.[5] The coal burning ovens produced ashes that had to be shovelled out into the street at regular intervals. With refrigerators a rarity, in summer the dough had to be carried out into the street 'to keep it from exploding', while its legendary toughness meant that bakers were known to knead the dough with their feet.

The union's ethos had been established by the men who had led it from the beginning and who were, in the 1950s, nearing the end of their working lives. Known as the 'old timers', almost all of them born outside the United States, they were tough men who played their regular games of poker with bravado. One of the union's lawyers remembers a lot of money being slapped down on the green baize: '"Put down $100 not $1!" is what they would tell me if I had a good hand.' Even their meals were macho: steaks thrown into the bagel oven; thick, sweet, stewed coffee and home-brewed whiskey. The old timers were legends to be treated with deference – even when reminiscing about them fifty years later. 'You never spoke to the old timers unless they spoke to you,' recalls a baker from the American-born generation. 'You didn't approach them. And they didn't look at you. Among themselves they spoke Yiddish. Their first question to you – in English – usually was: "Who're you related to?"'

Family was central to Local 338's identity. One of the smallest unions in the International, with little more than 300 members at its peak, the union restricted membership to sons, nephews and other relatives of existing members. As a result, relationships within the union were highly complex. A not atypical example was that of the baker whose father (another Local 338 member) died on the job and whose mother married another bagel baker who, in turn, was the nephew of one of the old timers and who also had a son and a son-in-law in the union! Membership was not, however, automatic for family members. One old timer's son tells of how he went to the union office every Thursday afternoon for six months before he was given a permit to learn how to work the oven, while another clearly remembers the minimum rolling speed he had to demonstrate – at least 832 bagels an hour, apparently – before he was let in. In fact, many old timers did not want their American-born sons to go into the industry, preferring them to get an education and graduate into a middle-class job. But as these sons returned from serving in the Second World War and then the Korean War, a good many of their fathers had to concede that it was difficult to argue against a manual job that paid more than working as a policeman or as a teacher.

Local 338 was more like a club or guild than a twentieth-century labour union, and the lists of attendees at any Local 338 function show the same surnames popping up again and again. Everyone knew everyone. And, as in medieval guilds, each baker had a nickname. 'King Kong' was 6 foot 5 inches tall and had long arms; 'Iron Mike' never got sick; 'Vulture' had a bottomless appetite; and so on. This kind of camaraderie fostered solidarity and loyalty among members. It also reinforced union discipline.

There were a number of different union officers, but the man who called the shots at Local 338 was the business agent. It was the business agent who assigned workers to shops and shifts; it was to the business agent that a baker called in sick, not to the bakery. The business agent held the key to a baker's earnings, schedule and commute – the key, in other words, to his life. For the apprentices (or 'learners' as they were known in Local 338) this meant that they were expected to show their mettle by working the most unpleasant shifts in a variety of bakeries across the greater New York area. It wasn't unusual for a learner to work at as many as twenty-six different jobs during his first year, even if it took him two hours by train and bus to get from bakery to bakery in the small hours of the morning in the dead of winter. For the more established bakers, competition became particularly fierce in the summer when the business agent decided which of them would be tapped to work up in the 'Borsht Belt' resorts of the Catskill Mountains. These were plum jobs, not just because of their pleasant location but also because of the annual slump in bagel demand back in hot and humid Manhattan. 'If the Business Agent didn't like you, you were dead,' snorted former union members. 'It was a one man union.'

The last old timer to hold the job of business agent was Benny Greenspan. No one interviewed for this book remembers a nickname for Greenspan that would have been used to his face, although they all have plenty of their own names for him – a 'tyrant' and 'little Caesar' were among the more polite terms used. Not for Greenspan the new-fangled ideas of official work sheets and transparency: 'everything,' apparently, 'came out of a little black book'. As the 1950s drew to a close, however, there was no reason for Greenspan to change his approach. Mechanisation seemed a remote possibility. His way of working had proved effective and brought success.

Ben Greenspan's Testimonial Dinner on 26 November 1958, organised by the union as a tribute to the man and his achievements, bore witness to the confidence Local 338 felt about the future. An upbeat and classy affair, it was held at the fashionable Roosevelt Hotel and was attended by over four hundred guests. The

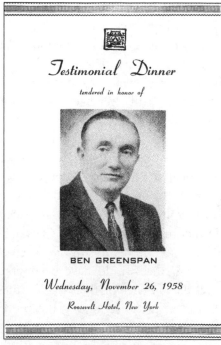

Testimonial Dinner

tendered in honor of

BEN GREENSPAN

Wednesday, November 26, 1958

Roosevelt Hotel, New York

30. Benny Greenspan was one of the founding members of Local 338 which celebrated its twenty-first birthday in 1958.

four-course meal boasted prime rib of beef with Baked Alaska for dessert. It was followed by a live variety show, compèred by the comedian Larry Alpert, one of the original cast of the 1951 show *Bagels and Yox.*

Outside the elegant confines of the Roosevelt Hotel, however, there was turmoil in the wider bakers' labour movement. In 1957, at the instigation of Robert F. Kennedy, then Chief Counsel on the

Senate's Permanent Subcommittee on Investigations, a Senate inquiry had been launched to look into corruption in the labour union movement. The principal focus of the inquiry was the Teamsters' Union, but the leader of the Bakery and Confectionery Workers' International, James Cross, did not escape a grilling by the senators and their young counsel. What that grilling revealed, as Kennedy wrote in his book *The Enemy Within*, was the sad story of an able man who 'became closer to the executives and officials of the companies that employed his union men than he was to his own membership. His initiative and ingenuity had deteriorated. He had developed rich tastes.'[6]

Cross's disgrace – his extravagant trips to Paris and his 'slim, dark haired and modishly dressed girlfriend' (who pleaded the Fifth Amendment in response to each question) – was played out in the national press and in front of the television cameras. Such damaging publicity was intolerable for America's foremost labour body, the AFL CIO, which had pledged to root out corruption among its members. Its response was to oust Cross and the B & C, just as it had ousted the Teamsters. Then the B & C itself split into two with the anti-Cross faction establishing a rival union, the American Bakery and Confectionery Workers (ABC) and taking a majority – 90,000 of the 150,000 strong membership – with it. Local 338 remained with the much diminished B & C, loyal to their New York vice-president Max Kralstein who had helped negotiate so many bagel contracts and who himself would remain loyal to Cross – at least for a few more years.[7] The Cross scandal and the ensuing bad blood in baker union politics may have seemed largely peripheral to New York's predictably stable bagel industry, but in time they would change forever the world in which the bagel bakers operated. New rivals were about to challenge Local 338's stranglehold on bagel production in greater New York.

*   *   *

By the early 1960s technology was beginning to catch up with bagel bakeries. The advent of the modern revolving oven accelerated the rate at which bagels could be baked. It also meant that the bagel bakeries could, at last, move out of their dingy cellars. The language of the contract signed between the union and the bakery owners in 1962 (which, significantly, was signed for two years and not one) was defensive, spelling out the need for the union to inspect the new so-called 'storefront bakeries'. There is an undercurrent of disquiet in the wording, despite the improved working conditions for the bakers. It was not just that the union was losing control; it was also the fact that, for the first time, bagels were being sold directly to the customers. Until now the cellar bakeries had sold their bagels wholesale to delicatessens, supermarkets and other bakeries. For the bakery 'bosses' of the Bagel Bakers' Association, the arrival of operations at street level was a business revelation. Consumers paid more than the retailer and could not get enough of the freshly baked *hot* bagel, something which had not been available in the days of wholesale. Blinking neon 'HOT BAGELS' signs were soon gracing the store windows of bakeries across the city. It was, says one baker, 'a bonanza'.

The bonanza was further fuelled by the fact that the bagel was, for the first time, attracting attention outside the Jewish community. Until now, only the *New York Times* had regularly

31. Neon 'Hot Bagel' signs started going up across New York in the 1960s.

mentioned the bagel, and inevitably mostly with reference to strikes by Local 338. That did not mean, however, that the *Times* assumed their readers knew what a bagel was. In more than one article the reporter had felt it necessary to provide definitions – 'glazed surfaced rolls with firm white dough' – as well as guidance on pronunciation – 'baygle'. The first culinary praise of the bagel in the mainstream American press appeared on 1 February 1958 in the *Saturday Evening Post*. Under the headline 'Secrets from My Mother's Kitchen' and next to a photograph of a spread which included chopped chicken liver, apple strudel and gefilte fish, as well as a few bagels, Sol Fox 'recalls the succulent master-pieces of his mother's table – and some of her best Jewish recipes'. More specifically, 'my favourite dishes on dairy nights were eggs scrambled with chopped onion, green pepper and lox, the smoked belly of the salmon: for a happy new taste experience, try a sandwich of cream cheese, sliced tomato and lox on a buttered bagel (doughnut shaped rolls boiled, then baked, to munchy firmness), our favourite Sunday breakfast.'

Predictably, this article and its welcome for the delights of Jewish cuisine did not go unnoticed by the *Jewish Bakers' Voice*. In an editorial entitled 'SATEVEPOST TELLS THEM WHAT'S GOOD', the excited baker bosses commented:

It is a universally accepted truth that the American way of life is an amalgam of many diverse traditions, customs, habits and beliefs. It is also accepted that this mixture has made America great. The Post article on traditional Jewish delicacies . . . is a good example of this truth. . . . Spaghetti and meat balls has [*sic*] ranked almost as a national favourite for more than a generation. The same is true for corned beef and cabbage. The latest additions to the American diet are our own blintzes, lox and cream cheese, gefilte fish and bagel.[8]

Soon entire articles were being devoted to the bagel. In 1961 it was featured in *Look* and in May 1963 alongside a profile of the movie star Shirley Temple in the popular American women's monthly *McCalls*. The *McCalls'* double-page spread was an enthusiastic stamp of approval.

> Join the stars below in this salute to Manhattan's most popular breakfast – bagels and lox. Bagels (in case you don't know them) are shaped like doughnuts and have a tooth-challenging chewiness. As for the taste of smoked salmon, you'll either adore it or hate it – nothing in between.

And the stars? Bagel aficionados ranged from Mrs Sam Levenson, wife of the comedian who quipped 'lox is Sam's caviar' to Jackie Gleason ('I lost weight eating bagels and lox. That was the year I just ate the hole') and, more surprisingly, the actor James Dean.

Bagel baking was turning into a golden business opportunity of which few bakers could have dreamt in the 1950s. Nor was it a coincidence that it was at this time that a number of bakers began to experiment with new flavours for bagels ('the old timers knew only plain and salt') and started to think about using bagels for sandwiches. Inevitably, all this attention on the bagel meant that more players were entering the market. Not all of them, however, wanted to play according to Local 338's rules.

'The beginning of the end,' remembers one Local 338 member, 'was Bagel Boys'. Bagel Boys was established in 1964 on King's Highway in Brooklyn, right in the heart of union-supporting Jewish New York. Having tried to no avail to sign up the shop, the union mounted a regular picket outside the bakery, a move which provoked a swift reaction from Bagel Boys' management: an intimidating phone call to one of Local 338's Executive Board threatening him, his wife and children with physical reprisals. The call was from one Sal Mauro, a man subsequently identified by a New York State investigation as 'Salvatore Passalaqua . . . well known to law enforcement agencies in the New York area'. In what was a perverse confirmation of the bagel's growing popularity, made all the more attractive for being a cash-in-hand business, organised crime was entering the bagel market.[9]

Mauro and his associates tried to argue with Local 338 representatives that they were 'special people' who should not be subject to the Local's uniform contract. When that failed they indicated that they would pay $10,000 for the union's 'cooperation'. Implacable against this kind of bribery, union members remember picketing the shop day and night, handing out free bagels to anyone who might have been interested in giving Bagel Boys custom, along with leaflets outlining the criminal background of some of the new bakery's owners. Bagel Boys finally backed down and signed a contract with Local 338.

No sooner had the Bagel Boys crisis been resolved than another, bigger challenge loomed. For the first time since the 1930s, bagels made by companies outside the greater New York area were coming into the city. The introduction of dough preservatives meant that for the first time bagels had a longer shelf life than five hours and could, therefore, be transported over long distances. The development – finally – of a working machine meant the out-of-town bagels were cheaper and, potentially, more numerous. When business agent Harold Laskowitz found out that a delivery was due to enter the city through the Holland Tunnel, he called up the Local's lawyer, Eugene Sosnoff, in a panic. 'What do you want me to do about it, Hal? Blow up the tunnel?' Laskowitz's answer – 'Can I?' – may sound like a jaunty rejoinder to the lawyer's sarcasm, but it betrayed genuine jitteriness. Apparently, Sal Mauro of Bagel Boys offered to 'solve' the problem. He or his cousin, he told union officials, could stop the bagels from coming in for 'fifty big ones' ($50,000).

Needless to say, nothing further came of Mauro's proposition. What the union did instead was to appeal to its customers. 'PLEASE DON'T BUY' was printed in bold letters on the leaflets distributed by Local 338 members in stores and markets. 'This out of state bakery is not subject to inspection by . . . City or State organizations charged with your protection.' Then came the emotional appeal to worker solidarity:

> the fight to obtain proper standards is New York is labor history. Stores, which in careless disregard of these facts sell Gourmet [the distributor] bagels, jeopardize the hard won standards of labor and inspection which the New York City public now enjoy.

The campaign got results. Consumers thought twice before abandoning the bagels they had been buying for years. Local

338 pressed home its advantage, taking the fight to Connecticut to one of the companies it considered a major culprit. The problem was that this particular culprit was already a union shop – but within the B & C's rival union, the ABC. The representatives of Local 338 soon determined that the ABC contract was 'substandard' and the wages on offer 'something below poverty levels'. Initially, it looked as if they had won when the National Labor Relations Board agreed that Local 338 should be able to offer these Connecticut workers representation.[10] But Local 338 could not establish a foothold in the factory: the workers stuck with the other union. Later that year, Local 338 took the unusual step of going to Washington, DC to picket the headquarters of the AFL CIO. Their protest, to anyone who would listen to them or read their printed leaflet, was that all the hard-won achievements of *their* union were threatened by another union's signing of substandard contracts with bakeries not only in Connecticut but also in New Jersey and New York. The larger point was that these employers in New York, Connecticut and New Jersey had *already* managed to agree contracts deemed substandard by Local 338. The bagel bakers' union had lost some key battles and the war against the machine was just beginning.

Back in New York the atmosphere inside Local 338 was, by all accounts, growing more and more heated as people started to realise that their way of work and life was under threat. 'It was boiling, boiling over! People were screaming their heads off at meetings [of which there were more than ever before]: "We will never let the machines into New York! When they bring the machines to New York we will picket them round the clock!" '

With hindsight it is easy to see that the march of the machine, advancing hand in hand with the increasing popularity of the bagel, was unstoppable. To speak out at the time in favour of working with machine shops, however, took considerable prescience and even greater guts. Morris Skolnick, son of Shymon, business agent Benny Greenspan's predecessor in the job, was consumed with the need to reform the union and change his fellow bakers' perspective. Skolnick was not afraid to call a spade a spade. He would have been aware of the simmering discontent within union ranks at the way union permits were given out almost exclusively to officers' relatives. He was demanding transparency and accountability and he was not afraid to make examples of fellow union members to prove his point. None of this made him popular: 'the more he showed up their fallacies, the more they disliked him'. But he cared deeply about the future of the union, and he was convinced that the future would have to include the machine. Skolnick's argument was that the union should organise machine shops. His proposal was to meet the bosses half way. His point – a prophetic one – was that the union was in danger of losing the whole industry if it didn't compromise with the machine.

Skolnick's suggestion was not without precedent. In Boston, the business agent of Local 45, George Newman, had done just such a deal. 'I saw the situation where the machine was going to replace hand labour . . . I made an agreement with the largest bagel baker in the Boston area to establish an hourly rate of pay reasonable from the employer's point of view and employees. And that system was very effective in maintaining peace between bakers and owners. There was no way that hand-made could compete with machine.'[11] Newman remembers trying to persuade Local 338's business agent Harold Laskowitz of the wisdom of this course of action. 'I said: "You can't compete, machine versus hand labour doesn't work." "Naah," said Laskowitz, "it doesn't work that way." They were arrogant . . . "We're the bagel bakers, they need us, they wouldn't dare." He went back to his bakers and said, "Aah, that blow hard from Local 45; we're not going to buy that."'

The argument made by both George Newman and Morris Skolnick was not one most members of Local 338 wanted to hear. They were earning a good living, a very good living. It seems that, unlike their fathers, many of them actually wanted their sons to go into the industry. Paradoxically, what made them perhaps even less willing to contemplate compromise with the machine was the fact that they had literally muscled and sweated their way to these good living standards. Twelve hours on one's feet rolling bagels and lifting huge tubs of dough year after year take their physical toll. 'I had worked too hard for this,' says one baker. 'My dad earned $68 a week, I was earning $300. I had a bad walk and arthritis as a result of working in the bakeries. I wasn't going to give this up.' It was hardly surprising, then, that when Skolnick ran for business agent on 16 March 1965 he lost, by 93 votes to 154.

It was at this point that many bakers began to abandon Local 338. 'I remember,' says Morris Skolnick's brother Terry, 'coming home one night from a union meeting and thinking [that] we have to leave while we still have a few dollars in the bank. My feeling was that it was going to go down. There was no way they were going to stop the machine. Good friends of mine from the local had gone to Baltimore and opened up a bagel shop. They were doing fabulous.' And so Terry Skolnick took out the *American Jewish Yearbook*, looked down the list of American cities with sizeable Jewish populations and moved to Cleveland, Ohio to a Jewish suburb where he was, apparently, an 'instant success'. And Skolnick was not the only one to take out his *American Jewish Yearbook*. The bagel bakers of Local 338 were voting with their feet and fanning out across the USA – Michigan, California, Colorado, Florida, Nevada – creating new markets for bagels and new devotees as they did so. Even a disillusioned Morris Skolnick would leave the union, although he didn't go far; he settled for suburban Long Island where he ended up operating one of the area's biggest wholesalers.

Tales of successful bagel ventures out West could hardly have been good news for morale back in New York, particularly in 1966 when the city was experiencing a traumatic period of financial crisis and crippling public service strikes. That same year an automated bagel factory, W & S, opened inside metropolitan New York, in the Bronx. W & S soon began undercutting the union-made, hand-rolled bagels by 10 cents a dozen, or over 15 per cent. The business was given a further boost by its association with the gangster John Dio, a man whose saturnine features and sharp suits had more than once been plastered across American newspapers. Dio arranged the distribution of the bagels and had contacts with supermarket buyers. Very soon after W & S's launch at least one supermarket chain replaced $3,000 to $4,000-worth of union bagels with W & S's machine-made ones. Although W & S would eventually go bankrupt, the point had been forcibly made. The bagel bosses were looking disaster in the face if they did not get machines and start reducing costs. On 1 December they threw down the gauntlet to the union. The list of demands they presented was radical – a 40 per cent wage cut, paid holidays down by a third and the number of workers on a shift halved.

An anonymous letter sent to B & C headquarters in Washington, DC and dated 12 December 1966 gives an indication of the despair and anger felt by those bakers still in the union. In a trembling hand unused, it would seem, to wielding a pen (or to writing in English), the message comes straight from the heart:

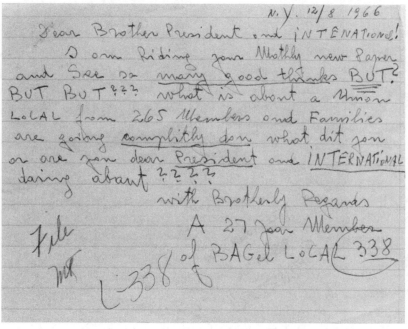

32. Note by an anonymous member of Local 338.

On 1 February 1967 the bosses shut the bakery doors. From their perspective they did this simply because they did not have enough work for the bakers. According to the union, the bosses were intent on 'destroying' their workforce. Immediately, the twenty-one bakeries in question were surrounded by union pickets. As with previous protests, customers were encouraged to see the union's point of view by being given free bagels if they did not cross the picket line. But, as one of the bakers recalls, this time the offer did not last long. There were logistical difficulties in delivering the bagels so that often by the time they arrived they were too hard to eat. The hand-outs were stopped. The dispute, however, showed no sign of stopping. And the pickets continued. It was clear that this dispute was serious. A lot was at stake on both sides. Certainly members of Local 3, New York's biggest B & C local, thought so and made their support known publicly – at least to begin with. Local 3 members were supplied with the addresses of affected bakers and urged to go down and join the picket lines in front of the bakeries.

But then there was silence. It is significant, and somehow poignant, that what would later be referred to as 'the big lock out', the dispute which 'changed everything', did not get any press coverage apart from a few notices from *Local 3 News*. Why? Because headlines such as the 1962 *New York Times*'s '85% BAGEL DROP IS SEEN IN STRIKE' were no longer relevant. Production was only slightly affected. Now supermarkets had other places to turn to for their bagels; now, too, for the first time there were reports of Local 338 bakers scabbing; and in the prosperous newly settled suburbs consumers had, it seemed, fewer qualms than workers in Brooklyn about crossing the picket line in front of their newly opened bagel outlets.

The only record of how the 1967 dispute ended is people's memories. 'It went on and on and on,' is how one baker remembers that spring and summer, 'and we kept walking and walking.' The majority of bakers went back to work some time in midsummer. Many of the shops left the union forever; those which stayed received unprecedented concessions from the union.

For the next few years Local 338 continued to limp along. There was still a demand for hand rollers since the machines were not yet completely reliable: one baker tells of having to resort to using a broom handle to keep the machine belt down; another recalls supermarkets complaining that the machine-made bagels were too small. But more and more of the better qualified people were leaving the union, often to open their own shops. By 1971 there were just 152 members remaining, and it seemed that the only way to keep the union alive – and the members' benefits going – was to merge with the much larger Local 3. Not everyone in Local 338 was convinced by this argument: 'We thought it was a sell-out. They weren't going to take care of us: they saw us as prima donnas. Their guys would go into the machine shops for less money.' But in the end the vote was unanimous if not uniformly enthusiastic. So on 1 July 1971 Local 3 acquired a Bagel Division and Local 338 ceased to exist.

Two months after the merger, the *Christian Science Monitor* ran a feature article about bagels.[12] 'It is no longer localized, nor ethnic, nor even handmade, as it was for centuries. . . . New York City alone now has over 100 bakeries that turn out nothing but bagels – at least

750,000 a day.' The bagel had, indeed, come a long way since Local 338's heyday in the 1950s. From thirty-odd bakeries to over one hundred, of which only forty were unionised; from one million bagels produced each weekend to three quarters of a million each day. From a bread unknown even to many New Yorkers to one which, according to the *Monitor*, prominently featured in the winning entry of 'Mrs Donald Wrede, a young matron of Cincinnati' in a 'best dressed table' competition. 'The centrepiece, placed on a black, amber and brown organic design tablecloth, was a basket filled with long spiky breadsticks and rolls of all varieties. She tied the napkin through the hole in the bagel resting on the bread plate – and won $1000.'

These were not developments that had been foreseen by either the old timers or, for that matter, New York's bagel bosses. The sting in the tail of the story of Local 338 is that its demise came not only with the machine but also as the popularity of the bagel was taking off.[13] Thanks to that popularity many sons of old timers would, as bosses of new retail bakeries across the US, go on to make a very good living. But it would take an outsider to Local 338 to 'think big' and bring the bagel well and truly into the American culinary mainstream.

CHAPTER 7

THE 'BAGELISING' OF AMERICA

'THAT'S BAGEL, B–A–G–E–L, A MIDWESTERN TREAT'
New York Times headline, 17 May 1986

One unusually cool summer morning in 2004, a small group of spectators gathered in front of an outdoor stage in the southern Illinois town of Mattoon where a talent show had brought together aspiring teenagers from around the region. An Elvis impersonator, a would-be soul diva, a violinist – all lined up to hear the verdict of the judges as it was broadcast live on local radio, as had been all their performances. The scene met all the expectations of a visitor to the Midwest: the friendly family atmosphere; the local reporter waiting, notepad in hand, for a comment from the talent show winner; the baseball diamond in the corner of the park. As the show concluded, the radio host reminded everyone that as well as the first, second and third prize winners, every contestant was entitled to a very special parting gift: a bag of bagels.

The prominent presence of the 'Jewish roll with a hole' in the middle of American corn and bean country may seem incongruous, but this talent show was – and still is – part of Mattoon's annual 'Bagelfest'. Since 1986 Mattoon has been home to the biggest bagel factory in the world, capable of producing three million bagels every day. If judged on volume alone then this small Illinois town has every right to claim that it, rather than New York, is the 'bagel capital of America'.

The bagel's road to Mattoon – and to Middle America – was built in the 1960s and 1970s. American eating habits were changing; machines were making bagel production faster and cheaper; America was, in the words of one observer, 'assimilating to the Jews'. These were, perhaps, necessary conditions, but they were not in themselves sufficient to guarantee the bagel nationwide popularity. What the bagel also needed was a champion. It was to find a tireless one in the Lender family.

*　*　*

Harry Lender had been a skilled, all-round baker back in Poland. When he landed in America in 1927 his first job was at a New Jersey bagel bakery, and it was in the bagel business that he would stay. Within the year, Lender had moved north to New Haven, Connecticut where he used his New Jersey savings to set up his own wholesale bagel bakery, one of a handful outside the greater New York area. By 1929 he had managed to bring over his family from Poland. All of them, wife and children, worked in some capacity in the bakery, even if it only meant threading twine through a dozen bagels and tying its two ends in a knot. It was

33. The Lender brothers in front of their new West Haven assembly line.

a decent living, although of limited potential: there were only so many bagels that the New Haven Jewish community (the numbers of which remained fairly constant from the 1920s to the 1960s) could eat.[1]

Ironically, it may be that the choice of this location, well outside the country's number one Jewish conurbation of New York, was the Lenders' first stroke of luck. In a smaller township, ethnic communities intermingled more, they shopped at each other's shops and ate each other's food. As the years went by, it became increasingly clear that the bagel was just as appetising to the Irish and Italians as it was to their Jewish neighbours. Slowly the business began to grow. Even so, the bagel remained mainly a weekend product which made for a difficult work schedule: with bagels going stale a few hours after baking, advance baking was out of the question. As the first American-born Lender son Murray recalled:

All hell broke loose from Saturday morning until Sunday morning. We would bake constantly – anywhere from 3000 to 6000 dozen because that's when everyone ate bagels. It was a 24-hour stretch where you did nothing but work. The house was in front so you could go in and grab a cup of coffee or a quick bite in between 'doughs' but you didn't dare take a nap.[2]

At this point Harry Lender took a crucial and, as it turned out, industry-changing decision: he bought a freezer.

Frozen bread had been the subject of a number of excited articles in the *Jewish Bakers' Voice*. Its contributors were excited because this new technology, they hoped, might solve the age-old problem of bread going stale. In 1935, cereal chemists took part in a trial: blindfolded, they were asked to try bread frozen for a week, then defrosted and bread freshly baked: 'the majority voted for the week old product, for aroma and flavour'. 'The baking industry,' concluded the journal with satisfaction, 'seem[s] likely to win a considerable advantage. Shipment of bakery goods to more remote points and better adjustment of supply and demand, with less waste, are possible benefits.'[3] Prophetic words for the bagel story, but to begin with the Lenders' freezer was there simply to help spread the workload over the week. 'It was born out of convenience, for manufacturing,' says Marvin, the youngest brother, who was then a teenager helping out after school.

However, the immediate and not insignificant benefit the freezer brought to the Lenders was free Sunday nights. Eventually they perfected the system so that they only needed to work a four- or, at most, five-day week. Defrosting the bagels the night before delivery, the Lenders continued to deliver them fresh to the retailers, who were none the wiser about the time the product had spent in the freezer. 'We held our breath,' recalls Murray, 'waiting to see what the customers would say, but no one said anything because they didn't know. So we said: "Gee, this is pretty neat".' And so it went on for two years, until someone forgot to defrost the bagels and they were delivered still frozen. To begin with the customers were furious, but after the initial shock had subsided, no custom was lost. Hardly surprising, when people realised that they had already been happily buying defrosted bagels for some time.

A critical testing ground for the Lenders' frozen bagels was the Concord, one of the legendary hotels in the Catskills. For an establishment with three thousand regular diners, a frozen bagel was an attractive proposition because it guaranteed a constant inventory. The Concord remained a major client for many years, not least because the Lender's bagel was a smaller than average product, a definite budgetary advantage for a hotel whose clientele, in the words of the grandson of the hotel's founder and son of the man who did the deal with Murray Lender, 'was known for overeating',[4] and would have spread more cream cheese and piled more slices of smoked salmon on a bagel with a larger circumference.

The Concord hotel may have represented an increase in the volume of sales, but it was primarily a Jewish establishment. The other innovation introduced by the Lenders at more or less the same time would prove a significant breaching of ethnic lines. By packaging fresh bagels in batches of six into polyethylene bags, the Lenders were aligning themselves with other supermarket suppliers. Plastic bags of bagels meant easy access for customers, better hygiene and, with the addition of a mould inhibitor, a longer shelf life. Now the bagel was on American supermarket shelves alongside household names such as Pepperidge Farm and Wonderbread. But how to get the uninitiated to try these new-fangled bread rings, let alone buy them? One ploy was to give them flavours which people associated with breakfast breads – the classic taste of Danish pastry or German coffee cake. Step forward, in the mid-1950s, one of the very first cinnamon raisin bagels. Onion bagels, too, soon became part of the Lender's repertoire. To drum up trade, elder brother Sam's wife, Lee, took to the road, setting up her table in the bakery section of supermarkets where she would hand out bagels spread with cream cheese. Homespun these techniques may have been, but they worked so well that supermarket sales kept on growing: by 1959, 50 per cent of Lender's sales were to supermarkets, while the annual sales figures had almost tripled since 1955. Now, at last, Murray could afford to draw a salary.[5]

Production, however, was limited by the fact that the bagels were still handmade. The Lenders had been on the lookout for a machine that would shape the bagel rings when they chanced across science teacher and inventor Daniel Thompson in California. Thompson, whose father was a bagel baker, had been experimenting with bagel machines for years. He had developed a prototype; now all he needed was the opportunity to take his equipment beyond the development stage. So it was that the very first Thompson machine was leased by the Lenders in 1963. It was a partnership which may have been brief and memories (particularly on the Thompson side) less than happy, but both parties agree that it was the work of Daniel, together with his brother Sam, the Lenders' chief dough maker, that revolutionised bagel making.[6]

The other crucial ingredient of that revolution was frozen food's seduction of the American consumer. Marvin remembers how he and his brother Murray closely followed the rising fortunes of Sara Lee's newly launched frozen cheesecake. 'It became clear that if you can take a cheese-cake, freeze it and make it available to people all over the country why don't we try that with the bagel?' says Marvin. 'So we went from freezing as a convenience to us to a marketing tool for the consumer. That was the beginning of the breakthrough because no matter what we did, we were limited with fresh bagels. With frozen there were no boundaries.'[7]

The brothers decided their first target market should be New York City, a decision, it has to be said, that contained more than an element of bravado. The power of Local 338 and the attachment of New Yorkers to their hand-made bagels meant that the barrier to entry was high. On the other hand, at least most New Yorkers were familiar with the product. This meant that the Lenders could promote what a frozen bagel had to offer: convenience and value for money.[8] This was a campaign for which the Lenders were well qualified. Described by one admirer as Mr Outside and Mr Inside, Murray and Marvin complemented each other: Marvin, the logistics and manufacturing supremo always on the look-out for ways to make the process more efficient and the cost lower; and Murray, the charismatic showman, who loved to talk about the 'bagelisation' of America. When initial sales pitches to the city's supermarkets failed, Murray took matters into his own hands. Jules Rose of Sloan's supermarket chain was one of the buyers who initially resisted the frozen bagel:

> So Murray walked into my office and said 'clear the desk'. Then he got up on the desk and started dancing. During this silliness he dropped his pants and on his underpants were the words 'BUY BAGELS'. As Murray chanted 'FROZEN BAGELS', the product ceased to be as important as the presenter. I agreed to take a minimum order.[9]

'Zany' is a word often used to describe Murray Lender's approach to sales. Zany and, ultimately, effective in an era before impersonal food conglomerates. 'Food industry people,' says Jules Rose, 'felt an affinity for each other then. You were out to make money of course but you also enjoyed yourself.' Personal relationships, in other words, made it that bit easier to take risks, risks like putting frozen bagels in supermarket freezers. To begin with, however, it looked like Rose had made the wrong call: the Lenders' bagels were not selling.

One problem, remarked on by Rose and, according to Marvin Lender, the subject of a regular stream of letters to the Lenders' New Haven office, was that people were cutting their fingers on the defrosted but still clammy and slippery bagel when they tried to slice it. Fists were metaphorically shaken and law suits were threatened. In response, the brothers came up with the idea of pre-slicing before freezing. Slicing the bagel at the factory presented an expensive operational challenge, but once the necessary equipment was developed it turned out that the Lenders had created a significant new product. For Jules Rose this was the marketing stroke of genius that would make all the difference: 'It was all about convenience; now you could pop the half-bagel straight from the freezer into the toaster.'

As the 1960s gave way to the 1970s, sales started to take off. For all the resistance to them among some New Yorkers – 'frozen bagels were repugnant to me' was a not atypical reaction – their convenience and price proved seductive. Even the mother of Local 338's lawyer became a regular customer. The fact that a 1969 *New York Times* article on price hikes chose to focus on the cost of meat and frozen bagels is an indication of the frequency with which the latter were now being consumed, and not only in New York City.[10] A quick survey of supermarket display advertisements in Ohio, Illinois and Pennsylvania for that year shows that frozen bagels were becoming an attractive item to shoppers, and not all of them were produced by Lender's.

*   *   *

The Lenders had only two main competitors in these years: Bagel Kings in Miami and Abel's Bagels in Buffalo. Bagel Kings directly challenged Lender's in New York City by undercutting them on price, but the puny size of their Florida-made bagels would prove their undoing. In 1970 Bagel Kings was fined for selling bagels which weighed less than advertised. 'Consumers should not pay more money for less dough,' punned the city's Commissioner for Consumer Affairs. Predictably, not long afterwards the company went bust. Abel's Bagels, however, posed a more serious challenge. Claiming to be the longest running bagel operation in the United States (they had been established in 1913), Abel's, like Lender's, took off as a company in the late 1960s. Despite the odd Abel bagel being sold in the Lender's backyard of Connecticut, the two companies seem to have agreed to cater to different regional markets, at least for the time being.

With regard to the American consumer, the Lenders and their competitors had transformed the bagel into a toaster product at a time when toasters had become a staple item in every American kitchen.[11] Frozen food was becoming integral to American eating habits as more women worked outside the home and the daily commute to the workplace put a premium on quickly prepared meals. Supermarkets began to expand the number of their frozen food display cases. Underlying this acceptance of frozen food was, of course, the growing dominance of the supermarket chains, especially in the expanding suburbs.

Adding to the attraction of the bagel was its increasingly heavily promoted nutritional value. The prominent 'NO

PRESERVATIVES' label on the Lender's freezer bag was beginning to pay dividends. Convenience, it turned out, could have a dark side. 'FOOD SAFETY A WORRY IN ERA OF ADDITIVES' read the front page headline of the *New York Times* on 9 November 1969. Ralph Nader, known to the American public for having successfully taken on the automobile industry over safety issues, accused the Food and Drug Administration of failing to protect the public from potentially dangerous chemical additives in food, and in 1970 members of the US Senate heard testimony that 'forty of the country's sixty leading dry cereals have little nutritional value'. The following year, the makers of Wonderbread were taken to task by the Fair Trade Commission for making false claims about their product. Subsequent years would see a slew of books on Americans' 'faulty food habits' and the importance of eating 'good' bread. *The Good Breakfast Book*, for example, called on its readers to 'restore breakfast to its rightful place' and proposed, among other things, a recipe for bagels. All this was, of course, welcome grist to the Lender's marketing mill.

* * *

By 1971 Lender's sales had increased to $2.25 million, but the overwhelming bulk of their bagels were being consumed on the Eastern seaboard. If the Lenders wanted to expand westwards they were going to have to create a market from scratch, or rather they were going to have to persuade their brokers to create a market. This, apparently, is where they were meeting resistance. The bagel was perceived, if it was perceived at all, as an ethnic speciality bread. As former Local 338 member Terry Skolnick found when he moved to Cleveland in the late 1960s, his retail shops in the suburbs did well but he could not get an appointment to speak with McDonald's and Burger King about making bagels for them: it was 'too Jewish' a product.

In one of the first feature articles about the family business, Murray Lender addressed the ethnicity issue head on. 'A bagel has versatility. When most people call it a Jewish product, it hurts us. It's a roll, a roll with personality. If you must be ethnic you can call it a Jewish English muffin with personality. You can use it for breakfast, sandwiches, TV snacks, dinner rolls – from morning till evening. We don't talk of bagels, lox (Nova Scotia salmon) and cream cheese. It limits them. Think of toasted bagels and jam, if you like.'[12]

This is a strangely defensive quote from Murray, who was normally anything but apologetic about his product and who, according to just about everyone interviewed for this book, would become one of the great food marketeers of his generation. What one senses in this early interview is a strategy in the process of formulation. Murray realised that the bagel's ethnic profile needed to be softened by associating it with familiar 'American' foods like the English muffin and jam. In time, hamburgers, tuna fish and even, unlikely as it sounds, bacon, would be used by Lender's to promote 'the Jewish English muffin', a description that would figure regularly in Lender's promotional literature.

One of Murray's more daring moves, and a logical if ambitious consequence of associating bagels with mainstream American foods, was to get the bagel cross-promoted with other food products which were already national brands. 'He was knocking on the door of General Foods when there wasn't a person there who knew what a bagel was,' remembers his brother Marvin. But once that door opened, Murray engineered deals with Dannon, Maxwell House, Smuckers, Minute Maid and, above all, Kraft and its Philadelphia Cream Cheese. These deals allowed Lender's to 'reward the consumers' by including coupons for jam, yoghurt or coffee in their bag of bagels and, in turn, encouraged the purchase of frozen bagels by printing Lender's coupons on the backs of fruit-juice cartons, coffee cans and tubs of cream cheese. The tie-up with Kraft gave Lender's, a small, relatively unknown company, the stamp of approval from a trusted brand. 'Philadelphia Cream Cheese had always been the leader. Its aura,' says Jules Rose, 'increased the quality of Lender's bagels.'

But there was still the critical matter of motivating the food brokers to get Lender's bagels into freezers across America. The man who would be Murray's artistic partner in the 'bagelising of America' was Willy Evans. Like Murray and Marvin, the son of Jewish immigrants from Poland, Willy had also grown up in New Haven, vaguely aware of Murray, a boy a few years younger than himself who worked at his father's bagel bakery and in his spare time made 'an extra buck' selling feathers and banners at Yale football games. As an adult, Murray came to rely on Willy's talent as a cartoonist, prevailing upon Willy to do the odd sketch in between running the family's supermarket. 'It's that bagel man again,' his secretary would complain as she buzzed Murray through. When in the mid 1960s Willy was suddenly without a job, he got a call from the Lenders suggesting he work with them

34. Willy Evans creates romance out of brand cross-promotion.

full time. 'It was a small salary and the office was tiny and hot since it was just above the bagel oven. They could barely pay their bills at the time,' remembers Willy. But from the beginning it was fun. Indeed, Willy's only condition for doing creative promotion for the Lenders was that he be able to poke fun at the bagel.

The first thing Willy did was to transform the three Lender brothers into cartoon characters – 'three little guys,' explains Willy, 'like [Rice Krispies'] Snap, Crackle and Pop' – and to write 'a little thing called the Lender's Bagel Story about growing up on Baldwin Street with the bagel factory at the back'. Now the company had spokespeople and a memorable visual message to convey to the brokers. 'We didn't have much money so we couldn't afford glossy brochures. Instead we handed out cartoons to the brokers. Cartoons with Murray jumping over a bagel and Sam looking behind another bagel. It was crazy. But it worked!' The family and the family's story soon became an integral part of the company brand.

35. 'The Dance of the Bagels', as performed by Lender's management.

The Lenders may not have been able to afford the cash prizes that other companies could hand out to their brokers but, arguably, far more memorable were the 'strange things' – as one victim of a Lender's prank puts it some thirty years on – that Murray, Marvin and their team would get up to at the annual gatherings of food brokers. Every year the Lenders would lay on a huge buffet – a 'smorgasbagel' – and their own variety show, starring themselves. One year they appeared in drag and another, trained by the creative director of the Connecticut Ballet, in tutus to perform 'the Dance of the Bagels'. Awards came in the form of a 'This is Your Life' celebration of popular brokers, with family, friends and, in one case, war buddies shipped in from around the country. These antics did not just endear the brokers to the Lenders, they cemented personal relationships, which made all the difference for a product that needed pushing. The point to remember, stresses Barry Ansel who came in as national sales manager in 1973 (and was promptly told that he had no sales staff), is that this was all done on a shoestring. It was creativity born out of a limited budget.

No avenue went unexplored; no initiative was too far fetched. For his son's Bar Mitzvah guests, Willy distributed varnished mini-bagels with painted-on faces as novelty gifts. Soon 'bagel-heads' were among the Lender company's most popular promotional material. Company directors lined up at trade fairs to have their likeness painted; secretaries were given bagel-head necklaces with their names on them; for a time bagel-head production became a business in its own right.

With the brokers on side, the Lender's frozen bagel began to roll out across America. In the early 1970s they won their first nationwide food service contracts with, among others, the hotel and restaurant chain Howard Johnson's. They were contracted to supply US military bases around the world. At the same time, diversification of the product was proceeding apace and not just in size and flavour. Lender's began to make private label bagels for supermarkets as well as partially baked bagels for the in-store bakeries and fresh baked for the in-store delis. They could, in other words, now sell bagels to four different outlets at the same supermarket. By 1975 they had opened a second plant in West Haven. The following year, Lender's bought Abel's Bagels (whose two factories by this time had the capacity to produce 1,700 bagels an hour) and, crucially, Abel's distribution networks. They were expanding so fast that, as Marvin Lender says, 'We were always undercapitalised. I spent most of my time borrowing money.' By 1977 Lender's could claim that their bagels were available nationwide.

*   *   *

The market for bagels was expanding at a time when the cultural mood of the country was changing. It was not just that anti-Semitism had ceased to be respectable, or that the Jewish community was growing in confidence. There was also, more generally, a shift away from the homogeneity and standardisation promoted in American popular culture in the 1950s and early 1960s. In the 1970s Americans were more interested in celebrating ethnic difference. The melting pot metaphor was being replaced by that of the cultural mosaic or, in culinary terms, the tossed salad. One reflection of this mood change was the 1974 Ethnic Heritage Act 'to support funding of initiatives which

36. Irving Fields's *Bagels and Bongos* sold over two million copies.

promote distinctive cultures and histories of ethnic populations'. As Marilyn Halter argues in *Shopping for Identity (The Marketing of Ethnicity)*, this new image of society had obvious implications for mass marketing. To be ethnic, or at least a little ethnic, was no longer a handicap; it could in fact be an advantage. The bagel, a product that was idiosyncratic but not too esoteric or too hard to pronounce, fit well into this category.

Bagels were creeping into American popular culture in a myriad of unusual ways. The pianist Irving Fields's 1959 album *Bagels and Bongos* featuring arrangements of Jewish melodies to Latin American rhythms, might have been dismissed by some critics as 'the monster of Jewzak', but it sold two million copies. Hollywood devoted a whole minute-and-a-half to a dispute between a sleazy nightclub impresario and a restaurant manager who, as the *New York Times* reviewer put it, threw 'bagels to the floor one by one with rage and elegance' in the 1969 film *The Night They Raided Minsky's*. Even the debonair Alistair Cooke chose to highlight the work of bagel bakers for an edition of his Emmy Award winning television programme *Omnibus* on New York's night workers.

And then there was the very special promotion of the bagel by the Israeli airline El Al. Having introduced bagels, cream cheese and lox as a signature dish on their Sunday morning flights to Israel, the airline executives soon realised that their non-Jewish passengers (about a third of all customers) had never seen a bagel in their lives. The marketing opportunity to include a branded booklet – *El Al Looks into the Bagel* – on the brunch tray proved irresistible. Here in fourteen small pages was everything one wanted to know about the bagel: the legends of its origin; tips on bagel etiquette ('grasp it firmly with both hands and pull apart with a twisting motion. Now pull a little harder. A little harder . . .'); what a person's bagel-slicing technique reveals about their character; and a bagel-ordering guide 'to help you eat bagels wherever you go'. Passengers wrote to the airline taking issue with the historical version presented. Such was the scale of interest generated that El Al established a Bagel Research

37. Bagels explained courtesy of El Al Airlines.

Center at its New York office. The *Saturday Review* magazine also entered the fray, first with an article about the booklet and then with a series of 'corrective' Letters to the Editor. *El Al Looks into the Bagel* proved a public relations masterstroke and was reprinted at least four times.[13]

Above all, though, it was professional comedians (an overwhelming proportion of whom were Jewish) who were dripfeeding the American public with bagel jokes on radio and especially television. For Molly Goldberg, bagel consumption was a family occasion:

> The bagel is a lonely roll to eat all by yourself because in order for the good taste to come out you need your family. One to cut the bagels, one to toast them, one to put on the cream cheese and the lox, one to put them on the table and one to supervise.[14]

Milton Berle provided no fewer than five separate bagel jokes in his *Private Joke File*, including this one:

> We used to buy day-old bagels. They were so hard we had to hammer the butter on. Then my uncle came up with a brilliant idea. He went to Israel and made a fortune selling Cheerios as bagel seeds. If you believe either of the previous there's some border property along the Golan Heights I'd like to sell you![15]

Even a young Woody Allen got in on the act, according to a bemused 1963 *Time* magazine article:

One of Allen's routines is premised on the axiom that people need taboo subjects. In the Faroe Islands, for example, where love-making is as casual as conversation, sleazy natives sidle up to strangers on street corners and try to sell them pictures of food. A piece of corned beef with just a little fat on it is considered very provocative. A girl is asked if she would like a little cream cheese with her bagels and she says: 'I don't do that kind of thing.'

Some of these jokes may have been 'kind of derogatory' as Murray Lender put it, but they 'helped present the product to the public'. The word 'bagel' was entering everyday American vocabulary, even at the Pentagon where officers used the word to describe the pattern of bombing that they were executing in Vietnam: 'You might call the whole thing a bagel strategy. We will bomb all around Haiphong and isolate it.'[16] The bagel was reaching cultural critical mass. Those people whose business it was to recognise trends were now willing to invest money in bagel products, however offbeat.

In 1974 Judith Hope Blau, artist and granddaughter of a Bronx bagel baker, made a bagel necklace for her young daughter. Within a few days of the necklace having caused a furore at her daughter's school, Blau had an order for 120 necklaces from Bloomingdale's department store. Her three-bedroom apartment became the base of a manufacturing business, the bathtub full of bagels stirred every few hours to keep them from going mouldy. Soon afterwards Judith was commissioned to write a children's book about her grandfather, the bagel baker. One of the first of a number of

38. The bagel as comedic prop: on *The Ed Sullivan Show* Jerry Stiller holds a bagel up to his partner (and wife) Anne Meara, as she does a shamrock to him.

bagel-themed children's books in America, *The Bagel Baker of Mulliner Lane* was a story which reflected the decade's greater ease with the cultural mosaic model of America. Ethnicity may not have been explicit, but the Yiddish rhythm of the bagel bakers' English – 'To a sack of flour dust, I am married. Who needs such a mess on her clean floors?' – and, of course, the object at the centre of the story, were gently and nostalgically Jewish. At the same time, crucial to the plot was the coming together of neighbours of different backgrounds to help Izzy the bagel baker on the 'special week' during which both Christmas and Hannukah happened to fall. Reviewed in the national press and on television, *The Bagel Baker of Mulliner Lane* proved sufficiently popular to convince the Fieldcrest linen company to launch, in 1977, one of their first 'designer' lines for children based on Judith Hope Blau's drawings. Blau remembers a certain apprehension at Lender's headquarters over the resemblance between her bagel characters and Willy Evans's 'bagel-heads'.[17] In fact, it was obvious that this coincidence could only be a good thing for both parties.

* * *

Hitherto the Lenders had focused their publicity efforts firmly on the trade, the brokers and supermarket buyers. By 1977 it was time to go straight to the public and invest in a television advertising campaign. 'Hello bagel lovers,' started every commercial. 'This is Murray Lender and as you can tell from looking [all three brothers would turn to show their profile], these are my brothers Sam and Marvin. On my left side is my brother Sam, and on my right foot is my brother Marvin.' The tone was wise-cracking ('We're in your grocer's freezer. Why, you ask? Because that's where we put them'); the humour slapstick (to the accompaniment of appropriate sound effects, Cartoon Murray shoots off a toaster as the bagel comes out and lands with the bagel in a basket) and the punch line homely ('a product of Sam, Marvin and me – from our family to yours'). First aired during the intermissions of Johnny Carson's *Tonight Show* in the late 1970s, their impact was undeniable: by 1979 Lender's was recording $22 million worth of sales. America was well and truly being bagelised. Bagel bakeries across the country, large and

39. Murray Lender on Johnny Carson's *Tonight Show* in 1977 to announce the national availability of Lender's bagels. Note Carson's bagel-head.

small, were experiencing increasing sales. Of course, this was not solely owing to the work of the Lenders, but almost every independent bagel baker interviewed for this book gives them significant credit for boosting the product's profile.

Back in the city that likes to think of itself as the home of the bagel, however, dissident voices were being raised. The main charge was that, as the bagel had pursued fame and fortune, as a food stuff it had changed beyond recognition. To begin with there were the voices of Manhattan bagel bakery owners, people such as Helen Katzman who refused to accept that a Lender's bagel was a bagel at all. 'How can that be a bagel? A doughnut dipped in cement and then frozen? It's strictly an imitation. . . . Machines don't make art.'[18]

Other consumers who did not wish to be named referred to the Lender's product as 'the bagel of last resort', grudgingly conceding that they bought frozen bagels to supplement the weekend purchase from the bagel bakery. The most serious criticism came from influential food critic Mimi Sheraton. 'Having visited twenty bakeries,' she wrote in *New York* magazine in 1973, 'and tried over 100 bagels from grocery stores I can safely and sadly report there isn't an old fashioned bagel to be had.'[19] And she reserved her particular ire for the frozen variety: 'frozen Lender's . . . bagels were mere jokes containing eggs and . . . vegetable shortening which made them like cakes.' The gloomy mood of critics like Mimi Sheraton only deepened as Lender's sales grew. Eight years later she was back on the offensive, this time bemoaning the work of bagel bakers on the East Side of Manhattan:

Certainly I had been aware of the decline in the craft of bagel making over the years but not even in my most pessimistic moments did I imagine it would come to this. What used to be a fairly small, dense, gray, cool and chewy delight that gave jaw muscles a Sunday morning workout had become snowy white, soft, puffy and huge and is now even served hot or worse yet, toasted. . . . Reasons for the demise of the bagel, like gigantic croissants, are not hard to fathom. The greatest cost in making either is the labor required; the cost of ingredients is relatively low. It therefore costs just about as much to make a small bagel . . . as to make a large one, but only larger sizes fetch high prices . . . Softness induced by dough conditioners and preservatives has to do with shelf life and *a public too lazy to chew.*[20] (author's italics)

The public was getting the bagel they deserved. Never having sampled the delights of the 'cement doughnut' which 'lies on your stomach at least five hours after being consumed', they preferred a fluffier, easy to digest, pre-sliced bagel which could be used to make sandwiches. This change was distressing for traditionalists and connoisseurs, but for the Lenders it was reaping rich rewards in terms of sales figures, the like of which they could not even have dreamed of ten years earlier. In 1983 the company registered $50 million worth of bagels sold; in 1984 the figure jumped to $65 million. That same year the brothers sold the company to Kraft, the makers of Philadelphia Cream Cheese.

It was billed 'the wedding of the century', and it took place in Tarpon Springs, Florida on a sunny September weekend. The 'congregation' was made up of all 120 Lender's brokers (and their wives), assembled together for the first time in light of this important event. The bride was Phyl, a tub of Philadelphia Whipped Cream Cheese given away by the president of Kraft's Retail Food Group. The groom, Len, an eight-foot bagel, was accompanied down the aisle by Murray and Marvin. After a trumpet fanfare, a 'justice of the peace' intoned: 'Dearly beloved, we are gathered here today to join this bagel and this cream cheese in wholesome matrimony. This is a natural relation, instituted by entrepreneurs and perpetuated by consumers. I now ask you both in the presence of the brokers to state your intentions. Have you come here freely and without preservatives?' Once the happy couple had exchanged their vows, the ever ambitious Lender brothers (who had agreed to run Kraft's new bagel division for the following two years), presented the company's sales plans. The scale of the Kraft distribution machine gave them new possibilities: according to one survey, 80 per cent of Americans had yet to taste a bagel in 1984.

The year was 1985 and bagel sales were at their highest ever. It was, however, also the year that Lender's (Kraft had maintained the name) was faced with its first serious competitor: Sara Lee, the company that had been the original inspiration for the brothers to 'think big'. Sara Lee had been one of the companies eager to buy Lender's. Turned down but privy to information they had gained when they formally evaluated the company and its prospects for acquisition, they decided to invest heavily in developing their own brand of frozen bagel. The resulting 'holey wars' were to push up retail sales of frozen bagels, Murray claimed, by 30 per cent. Certainly, the nation's awareness of bagels could only have been significantly heightened by the animated Lender brothers' commercials – 'from our family to yours' – running head to head on television with the multi-Grammy-winning jazz musician Al Jarreau jamming a Sara Lee bagel jingle and telling the audience: 'It's not just a piece of bread, you dig?'

By 1986 total sales of bagels in the United States were expected to hit the $500 million mark. Of these bagels 40 per cent were frozen, with Sara Lee representing 6 per cent of all sales against Lender's 34 per cent. Despite its still dominant position, however, Lender's and Kraft were finding it difficult to meet growing demand. Their factories in Connecticut and New York did not have the capacity to turn out bagels fast enough – especially for the Midwest where consumption was predicted to grow twice as quickly as the national average. The answer to the problem was obvious: open a plant in the Midwest. So in May 1986 the world's biggest bagel factory, designed by Marvin Lender, was officially opened in Mattoon, Illinois.

* * *

Capable in 1986 of churning out a million bagels a day, the Mattoon plant was record-breaking by any measure. But its establishment in Mattoon also had huge symbolic significance. This was the first major bagel bakery in corn and bean country: most Mattooners had never eaten a bagel, let alone made one. The bagel had landed in the heart of middle America. And it was welcomed with open arms, not only because it provided hundreds of jobs but also because its exotic nature would result in the bagel becoming the town's main tourist attraction.

In 1986, at the Lender brothers' instigation, Kraft decided to host 'the World's Biggest Bagel Breakfast' to introduce Mattoon townsfolk to this bread ring which was now such an important part of their economy. Thousands of people – 'they came straight from the farms', marvelled Willy Evans – crowded Broadway Avenue to sit down at one of the red-and-white checked cloth-covered tables which stretched over two city blocks and have a cup of coffee and a bagel with cream cheese, all courtesy of Lender's. Staffed by volunteers from the town, the breakfast proved a huge success, so much so that a committee of community leaders decided to use the bagel to promote tourism to Mattoon. Neighbouring towns had festivals based on cheese and broom corn; Mattoon would have the 'Bagelfest'.

The irony of all of this is that bagels may not, after all, have been so very strange to Mattoon. Mattoon is not a typical prairie town; it is a railway town, which 'exploded into being' (as one local historian writes) because of the crossing of two railway lines in 1855, one of which would turn into the main Chicago to New Orleans line. Mattoon, as its tree-lined residential avenues attest, quickly grew prosperous thanks to the railway and the rich farmland surrounding it:

> Where the steeds of these great iron highways meet
> To unload the wealth of the world at her feet
> The Queen of the Prairie reclines on her throne,
> Receiving the tributes of every zone.[21]

A notable omission in the many articles about Lender's arriving in Mattoon is that a number of the town's first merchants were

40. Mattoon's very first 'World's Biggest Bagel Breakfast' in 1986.

Jewish. One of Mattoon's most eminent bankers, a man whose house is singled out in local guidebooks as the town's best example of the Queen Anne style of architecture, was Jewish. Indeed, in the 1950s and 1960s the *American Jewish Yearbook* listed Mattoon among its 'communities with a Jewish population of 100 or more'. So it is not inconceivable that at some point in Mattoon's history bagel baking was taking place in the privacy of certain kitchens. Nor is it out of the question that in the days when trains between Mattoon and Chicago were frequent, bagels were occasionally bought as treats in the big city for children back home.

The only person less than enthusiastic about the Lenders' arrival in Mattoon was, in fact, a member of the town's Jewish community.[22] His reason was simple. He saw the Bagelfest as an opportunity to celebrate Mattoon's Jewish heritage. When there was a discussion about which musical acts might be performed at the fest, he suggested a klezmer band; what was booked was a gospel group. It is not clear who took the decision to keep Jewishness out of the event, Kraft or the Mattoon town council. What is important to this story is the milestone this decision represented for the bagel. It had now formally shed its ethnicity. The bagel had become all-American.

POSTSCRIPT
THE BAGEL BITES BACK

Is twenty-first century America, then, truly 'bagelised'? Bagels are now available in virtually every supermarket, on every city street and at every airport in the country. They have their own category in the Department of Commerce's *US Industrial Outlook*. The inexorable rise in bagel consumption, however, seems to have peaked. So far, 2001 was the year with the highest sales. As for frozen bagels, they are definitely on a downward trajectory as consumers increasingly opt for the fresh variety. And bagel makers everywhere pale when celebrity diets make concerted attacks on carbohydrates. The industry's response, a 'low carb' bagel, does not seem to have had much impact, a fact which may be disappointing for the big manufacturers, but which, from an aficionado's perspective, is a positive sign.

As for Lender's Bagels, the business has weathered all these changes. It remains an industry leader and among the top five manufacturers of bagels, both frozen and fresh. It has also, however, had five owners in the space of twenty years. It last changed hands in February 2007 when it was bought by Blackstone, a Manhattan-based private equity firm. In an ironic coda to the Lender's story, it is now in the vanguard of American companies owned partially by the Chinese government.[1]

Needless to say, the rags to riches story of the American bagel has inspired scores of entrepreneurs to open bagel bakeries around the world. New York bagels are now available and popular in such unlikely places as Tokyo, Guangzhou and Buenos Aires. With all the razzmatazz of Hollywood the American roll with the hole has conquered new markets across the globe. But local cultures sometimes fight back. Bagel history is not dead and not every bagel tale ends in victory for the American interloper. This book, in other words, would not be complete without lightning visits to Montreal, London and Kraków.

＊　＊　＊

The vexed question of authenticity lies at the heart of the bagel story in Montreal, from the fraught issue of who exactly opened the first bagel bakery in the city to recent disgust at the New York bagel making inroads into the Canadian market. Press coverage of the American arrival was unabashedly emotional. 'Bagelville . . . plans to introduce New York style bagels . . . and is advertising itself as the best in town,' wrote Montreal's *Gazette* in 1995. 'It takes moxie [courage] to say that. But these guys need it now that they have entered the lion's den.' The language of the Montreal correspondent of the *Globe and Mail* was even more extreme: the opening of this bakery was quite simply 'sacrilegious'.

The tone of both articles is not simply a reflection of general attitudes in Canada towards its neighbour to the south. Montreal is home to a proud bagel tradition which began at about the same time as New York's, with the arrival of Jewish immigrants from Eastern Europe in the early 1900s. To this day the city's two landmark bagel bakeries, the St Viateur Bagel Shop (first owned by Hyam Seligman) and the Fairmount Bagel Bakery (established by Isadore Schlafman), continue to vie for Montreal's 'original bagel' crown. Irwin Schlafman, Isadore's grandson, insists that it was his grandfather who introduced the bagel to Montreal in 1919, even though this seems an implausibly late date.[2]

The debate over 'the original Montreal bagel' reveals something of Montreal's Jewish experience. A very different city from Manhattan, here the Jews were caught between the English ruling class and the French majority; membership of neither was available and the Jewish community was, in consequence, more inward-looking – dynamic but also defensive. In these circumstances the badge of authenticity takes on greater significance. The bagel trade, in fact, took a steep dive after the Second World War when the children of immigrants moved out of 'the Main', the old Jewish neighbourhood, to the leafier suburbs. It was by no means clear that bagel making would survive. Isadore Schlafman's son Jack, for example, quit the business altogether and went to work as a cutter in the garment trade. Meyer Lewkowicz, the Holocaust survivor who inherited the St Viateur bakery from Hyam Seligman, continued to keep the shop open for his regular, almost entirely Jewish, clientele, but he was a long way off realising his dream of buying a Cadillac.

'It was Don Bell that put us on the map,' recalls Joe Moreno,[3] the Italian Canadian who started making bagels alongside Lewkowicz at the age of twelve and who now owns St Viateur. Certainly, the popularity of Donald Bell's 1972 book *Saturday Night at the Bagel Factory and Other Montreal Stories* helped the bagel make the transition into the non-Jewish mainstream. 'Montreal is a Saturday city,' writes Bell in his introduction. 'On Saturdays, the whole city begins to tingle.' After paying homage to, among others, the Bistro Anti-Riot Squad and Nick the Greek's Greek Pool Room, he arrives at the Bagel Factory:

> But Saturdays belong most of all to the all-night bagel bakers in the all-night bagel bakery on St Viateur Street, to darling Mrs Riva Ruppel and to Joe and Jerry and to Mr Lewkowicz. Hot fresh bagels tumbling out of the oven, like Jewish halos – the fragrance of life!
>
> Of course any day of the week is good in Montreal. But Saturday is best. Get off the ship on a Saturday. And go to the bagel bakers.[4]

Soon Mr Lewkowicz ('a short but sturdily-built man with red hair and big ears that stick out below his Glenora Flour hat') and his bagel factory were familiar to thousands of Canadians across the country. His bakery's fame would spread further in 1974 when 'the Main' played host to a film crew recreating 1948 Jewish Montreal for the movie version of Mordechai Richler's best-selling *The Apprenticeship of Duddy Kravitz*. Billed as 'one of the most important films in Canadian history', it included a short scene in which Kravitz, played by Richard Dreyfuss, goes into a bagel factory remarkably similar to that of St Viateur. As Meyer Lewkowitz said in a 1990 television interview, 'Duddy Kravitz, this brings me business, the other book too [Don Bell's] and then television . . . it changed my life.' Five years later Irwin Schlafman purchased the property his grandfather Isadore had once owned, dusted down the still-standing oven complete with a blackened and petrified bagel, and re-opened the family business, calling it 'the *original* Fairmount Bagel Bakery'.

41. In the film version of Mordechai Richler's novel *The Apprenticeship of Duddy Kravitz*, Duddy (played by Richard Dreyfuss) grabs a bagel.

The 'authentic' Montreal bagel – a sweeter, less chewy bread than its New York cousin thanks to the malt and eggs in its dough – has prospered ever since. There is not a sliver of stainless steel in either the St Viateur or Fairmount bakeries. Their bagels are rolled by hand; the ovens are wood-burning and never shut down; the hot bagels are tipped out into a long, wooden trough set at an angle, rolling down slowly to the cash register and the customer at the head of the queue. American food critics such as Phyllis Richman of the *Washington Post* have given their emphatic seal of approval: 'the best [bagels] in the Western Hemisphere are from Montreal, not New York'.[5] Today, the Montreal bagel is having the last laugh *vis à vis* its New York cousin as, after years of machine-made bagels, the hand-rolled item begins to stage a come-back in Manhattan.

* * *

The British bagel is a diffident product, a fact which perhaps confirms its Britishness. There has been no outrage expressed in the local press at the arrival of American-style bagel chains which now pepper the city streets and railway stations, nor was there any public response to these chains' claims that they were 'introducing' the bagel to the UK. In fact, the British bagel has just as venerable a pedigree as its Montreal and New York cousins.

For many East European Jews, Britain was meant to be a staging post on the way to America, but thousands of them decided not to embark for the second leg of the journey. Most of these refugees settled in the 'sordid and shifty poverty'[6] of London's East End, where the Jewish population tripled between 1881 and 1914. Overwhelming the country's existing Jewish community,

the East Europeans were to set the culinary tone of Anglo-Jewry.
Bagel pedlars were soon a common sight in the East End, eking
out a living amid the clamour and mud of Petticoat Lane, Brick
Lane and Whitechapel.

In 1930s' London, one woman bagel pedlar became the inspiration for a bleak musing on death by the Yiddish poet Abraham
Nahum Stencl.[7] Here the bagel hole, far from being the precious

42. This woman bagel-seller in Whitechapel, pictured here in 1938, was almost
certainly the inspiration for Abraham Stencl's poem.

commodity avidly sought after by the Fools of Chelm, is omnipresent because it represents death and 'death is always there'. The bagel seller herself is described in graphic terms: 'her outstretched bony hands . . . from her consumed eye-sockets/peers a swollen tear and not an eye'. She is part of the well-established East End ritual of buying a bagel from the basket of a pedlar after attending synagogue. Stencl, who came from Poland and subsequently escaped the Nazis in Berlin, wrote these words in 1940, on the eve of the Holocaust. After the war he would champion Whitechapel as 'the last *shtetl*' and berate the Jews who had moved to more prosperous areas of London and become Anglicised.[8] But Stencl was in a minority. Most people wanted to leave:

> An English Jew travelling the world will be asked by the diamond magnate in Johannesburg: is the bagel woman with the upturned orange-box for a stall still at her pitch in the lane? . . . Whitechapel is a place where everyone was proud to be born – but nobody wants to live.[9]

From the early twentieth century, Jewish community leaders in Britain had been intent on passing on 'Anglo values' to the newly arrived Yiddish speakers from Eastern Europe, in 'ironing out', as the *Jewish Chronicle* put it, 'the ghetto bend'. As the underground train network extended its tentacles across the Thames Valley, so the Jews who could afford to moved north and east. Already by 1930 two thirds of London's Jews lived outside the Whitechapel area. The migration accelerated after the Second World War – and they took their taste for bagels into new, tree-lined Jewish neighbourhoods. Today there are thriving bagel bakeries (often run by Israelis) in places such as Golders Green, Hendon and Stoke Newington, but they have rarely expanded their business beyond their locality. British bagels have remained, on the whole, a bread apart. It is for this reason, perhaps, that the bagel continues to act as a badge of ethnic identity in Britain. In the 1930s the students of the East End's Jewish Free School were affectionately known as the 'bagel boys' because of the ring of yellow made by the gold ribbon stitched around their hats. Seventy years later, in the novel *Bagels for Breakfast*, bagel eating is one of the hurdles the Jewish hero's gentile girlfriend must surmount before being accepted, while a leading Jewish journal chooses the bagel as the object best representing Jewishness.

Ironically, two bakeries on Brick Lane are now the most prominent proselytisers of the merits of the British 'beigel'.[10] Since the 1960s the East End of London has been predominantly Bengali. Brick Lane is awash with curry houses, purveyors of a dish which has conquered the British stomach much as the bagel has the American one. The twenty-four-hour Beigel Bake at number 159 and Beigel Shop at number 155 are among the few vestiges of the area's Jewish past, and have become something of an institution, frequented by night-shift workers, bleary-eyed clubbers and movie stars. The actor and playwright Steven Berkoff writes of stopping off to buy still-warm bagels after performing in *The Glass Menagerie*:

One might chance to witness at the back of the shop sinewy men with coils of dough, appearing almost to wrestle with them in the manner of that great Greek legend Laocoon, where

43. Brick Lane, London.

we see a Herculean figure wrestling with what seems to be a giant anaconda. At that time of night the bagels are still warm. The flavour of a warm bagel is sensually delicious beyond all expectation.[11]

In comparison, writes Berkoff, 'America . . . changes beigal [sic] to bagel, doubles the size, reinvents it, muscling up the slim Euro bagel and flavouring it to a wild diversity for the ceaselessly unsatisfied Yankee palate . . . in New York the bagel has become the musical, it's all "tits and ass".'[12]

* * *

And so to Poland. Poland, where the baking industry had been heavily reliant on the Jewish community until 1939 and whose Jewish citizens and Jewish traditions were almost entirely wiped out by the Nazis. After the war it was above all in Kraków, one of the few cities to escape wholesale destruction, that bagels or *obwarzanki* started to be sold again. In the 1950s, privately owned bakeries in the city received something of a boost from the communist authorities, perhaps because Kraków's party leaders were more tolerant of small, private enterprises like bakeries, or because they were worried that state factories could not supply enough bread. One of the presumably unforeseen consequences of this policy was that Kraków once again became the bagel capital of Poland. Visitors from Warsaw or Gdańsk or Poznań were often asked to bring back for friends and relatives *krakowskie obwarzanki* or *bajgieł*, bought from one of the pushcarts stationed around the old town. So powerful is their reputation

44. In 2008 one of Kraków's fashionable food shops used a photograph from the 1930s of a boy peddling bagels on its shopping bags.

that it is sometimes difficult to convince people from Kraków that bagels were ever made anywhere else in the country.

At last count there are fifteen *obwarzanek* bakeries in Kraków. There is also an American-owned establishment in Kazimierz, the city's Jewish district, which specialises in burritos and bagels. A poster inside the café explaining what a bagel is makes one reference to its Polish antecedents: 'to some extent similar to the Polish pretzel . . . the bagel is one of the most popular breads in America'. And this hangs on a wall in a town where Jewish elders ruled on the value of the bagel in 1610 and around the corner from where one of the Beigel family bakeries was located before the Second World War. Although many Poles have used the words *bajgiel* and *obwarzanek* interchangeably for years, it seems that an insurmountable gap is in danger of opening up between the two and with it an opportunity missed for an exploration of a shared history. Of course, it is legitimate to argue, as a group of Kraków bakers do, that the Kraków *obwarzanek* is a significantly different product from the bigger, plumper and softer 'New York-style bagel' and is, because of its rich and long history, deserving of classification as a protected regional product by the European Union. But it is indisputable that the two are related, just as it is incontrovertible that the history of Poland cannot be separated from the history of its Jewish community.

*　*　*

As for the American Jewish community, so many of whom trace their roots back to Poland, many of their number are ambivalent about the bagel's resounding success. An atypical view is that expressed by the scholar and statesman Rabbi Arthur Hertzberg when he mused, 'How to affirm oneself as a Jew and an American?' and answered: 'We needed to contribute to America something other than bagels and Borscht Belt humor.'[13]

Over the course of the twentieth century, the bagel seems to have acquired the status of a touchstone of Jewishness within the American Jewish community – and not necessarily in a positive sense – as the children and grandchildren of Jewish immigrants moved out to the suburbs and assimilated into mainstream American culture. Bagels, or rather the combination of bagels and lox on a Sunday morning, became a dismissive shorthand for people who had only a superficial link with their Jewish identity. As early as 1976 Irving Howe commented that those who sneered at 'bagel and lox' Jewishness

> failed or preferred not to grasp that certain pinched qualities of suburban Jewish life – residual attachments to foods, a few customs, and a garbled Yiddish phrase – might signify not merely self-serving nostalgia but also blocked yearnings for elements of the past that seemed spiritually vital . . . 'bagel and lox' (not to be sneered at in their own right!) were part of what they still had left.[14]

The anthropologist Stanley Regelson took the defence of the bagel's reputation several controversial steps further in his analysis of the act of eating bagels with cream cheese and lox.[15] He argues that the combination of lox (red and therefore female) and cream cheese (white and therefore male) on a bagel 'can be seen as a reference not only to the breaking of the surface taboo . . . but a violation of the incest taboo itself'. And since, when the Messiah comes, 'the laws that govern the temporal world will cease to hold', those consumers of bagels and lox on a Sunday are actually unconsciously expressing their Jewish religiosity and Jewish ethnic identity.

Whether Regelson is right or not, the fact is that his words had a greater resonance when they were written, over a quarter of a century ago, at a time when the bagel still had a strong Jewish identity. Today, if there is an 'ethnic' identity attached to the bagel inside America it above all resides in New York City – often, as in the case of the current Lender's logo, simply alluded to pictorially in the outline of a Manhattan skyline. And yet, for all the shedding of its ethnicity in Middle America, the bagel continues to hold a certain fascination for the American Jewish community, one which is partially explained by the bagel's triumphant assimilation into American culture and all the complex feelings that assimilation provokes among American Jews. But it is more than that. It comes back to the bagel's shape and the layers of meaning that can be found in the ring with no beginning and no end, and in the hole which, as the Yiddish poets mused a century earlier, intimates both emptiness and eternity. The bagel, in other words, will not disappear from American Jewish culture just because of its commercial success. As just one example of many, let us examine the words of a Stamford, Connecticut rabbi on the eve of the new millennium.[16]

'Why,' he asked in his New Year sermons, 'does [the bagel] stand out, at least among Ashkenazi Jews, as the quintessential

Jewish food? And then it hit me. It's the hole.' And so he continues, for four sermons, arguing that the hole is not just about 'the yearning, the hunger, the dissatisfaction, the fear, the emptiness, the depression, the anger and the mortality'. The significance of the hole, what makes it Jewish, is also how it is filled. A hole can be a tragedy, but, 'we arise from the shiva [mourning] bench and remember our dead not with endless bitterness and regret but with . . . acts of kindness . . . not to deny tragedy – rather to grow from it.' The bagel's roundness is about inclusiveness – 'the Jewish ideal of the synthesis of alone and together'. 'Round foods,' concluded the rabbi on the Day of Atonement, 'that's our response to blood and swastikas. A delicious honey dipped challah. And a bagel with a hole.'

NOTES

Chapter 1 The Family Tree

1. Leah W. Leonard, *Jewish Cooking* (New York 1949).
2. Harold McGee, *McGee on Food & Cooking, An Encyclopedia of Kitchen Science, History and Culture* (London 2004), p. 521.
3. Usually 45 parts water to 100 parts flour, compared to a typical loaf's 65 parts to 100. Author's interview with New School baking instructor Lyn Kutner, New York, December 2004.
4. Stati di Ancona 1397. Author's interview with the Puglia-based food historian Guiseppe Fumarola in Martina Franca, September 2004.
5. Author's interview with bread scientist Stanley Cauvain, England, January 2005.
6. D.E. Bath and C.R. Hoseney, 'A Laboratory-Scale Bagel-Making Procedure', *Cereal Chemistry* Vol. 71, No. 5, 1994.
7. Gillian Riley, *The Oxford Companion to Italian Food* (New York 2007).
8. H.E. Jacob, *Six Thousand Years of Bread* (New York 1997), p. 164.
9. John Cooper, *Eat and Be Satisfied (A Social History of Jewish Food)* (Northvale, NJ 1993), p. 78.
10. Indeed, according to Cecil Roth, the first European Talmudist of note was from Puglia. Cecil Roth, *History of the Jews of Italy* (Philadelphia, PA 1946), p. 288.
11. Cyril D. Robinson in *Petits Propos Culinaires* (London 1992).
12. Gillian Riley, *Renaissance Recipes* (San Francisco 1993), p. 62.

13. Christofaro di Messisbugo, *Libro Novo* (Venice 1557).
14. This verse and other Tuscan visual references are from Giovanna Giusti Galardi, *Dolci a Corte* (Florence 2001).
15. Maria Dembińska, *Konsumpcja Żywnościowa w Polsce Średniowiecznej* (Wrocław 1963).
16. Jan Rutkowski, *Histoire Économique de la Pologne avant les partages* (Paris 1927).
17. Irene Krauss, *Gelungen geschlungen. Das grosse Buch Brezel. Wissenwertes. Alltagliches. Kurioses* (Tübingen 2003).
18. Irving Pfefferblit, 'The Bagel', *Commentary* Vol. 11, No. 5, May 1951.

Chapter 2 Of Bagels and Kings

1. The accepted version of the 1494 episode has been that the Jewish community was banished from Kraków by the Polish king. But recent scholarship reveals a more complex story. It may well have been advantageous to both the king and the Jewish community for the latter to resettle in Kazimierz. Further discussion can be found in Bożena Wyrozumska, 'Czy Jan Olbracht Wygnał Żydów z Krakowa?', *Rocznik Krakowski* (Kraków 1993) and Hanna Zaremska, 'Crossing the River: How and Why the Jews of Kraków Settled in Kazimierz at the End of the Fifteenth Century', *Polin* 2008.
2. Information cited in the Kraków Bakers' Guild submission to the European Union for the classification of the *obwarzanek* as a regional product, 23 October 2006.
3. H.H. Ben Sasson, *A History of the Jewish People* (Cambridge MA 1969), pp. 641–2.
4. Janusz Tazbir, *Kultura Szlachecka w Polsce* (Poznań 2002), p. 63.
5. Janusz Tazbir, *Państwo bez stosów i inne szkice* (Kraków 2000), p. 148.
6. The Karaites are a Jewish sect that came into being towards the middle of the ninth century. Their doctrine is characterised primarily by the denial of the Talmudic–rabbinical tradition (from the *Encyclopedia Judaica* (2007), Vol. II, p. 785.
7. Cited in Paweł Fijałkowski, *Dzieje Żydów w Polsce XI–XVIII wiek* (Warsaw 1993), p. 87.
8. Moses of Narol cited in *ibid.*, p. 51. Moses of Narol would become Rabbi of Metz, France.
9. Dr Bernard Connor, *The History of Poland in Several Letters to Persons of Quality* (London 1698).

10. Stefan Gąsiorowski has written in great and interesting detail about Christian–Jewish relations in Żółkiew at the time of Sobieski; see his *Chrześcijanie i Żydzi w Żółkwi w XVII i XVIII wieku* (Kraków 2001).

11. Adam Kaźmierczyk, 'Jakub Becal: King Jan III Sobieski's Jewish Factor', *Polin* Vol. 15, 2002.

12. Majer Bałaban, *Historia i Literatura Żydowska* (Lwów/Warsaw/Kraków 1925), p. 316.

13. Maurycy Horn, 'Król Jan III i Żydzi Polscy', *Biuletyn Żydowskiego Instytutu Historycznego* 1983, nr 4/128.

14. Veronica Belling, ' "Ahavat yehonatan": A Poem by Judah Leo Landau', *Polin* Vol. 15, 2002.

15. An interview with Philip Kraus in the American Jewish Committee Oral History collection at the Special Collections, Schaffer Library, Union College.

16. François Paulin Dalérac, *Polish Manuscripts of the Secret Histories of the Reign of John Sobieski* (London 1700), p. 68.

17. Janusz Tazbir, *Kultura Szlachecka w Polsce* (Poznań 2002), p. 155.

18. Cited in Bernard Lewis, *What Went Wrong?* (Oxford 2001), p. 16.

19. Muzeum Narodowe w Warszawie, *Chwała i Sława Jana III w Sztnce i Literaturze XVII–XX* (Warsaw 1983).

Chapter 3 Rituals, Rhymes and Revolutions

1. Majer Bałaban, 'Die Krakauer Judengemeinde-Ordnung von 1595', *Jahrbuch der Jüdische-Literarischen* (Frankfurt 1913). I am indebted to Barry Davis and to Professor Dovid Katz, Director of Research at the Vilnius Yiddish Institute of Vilnius University, for their translations of this text.

2. Jacob Rader Marcus, *The Jew in the Medieval World. A Source Book 315–1791* (Cincinnati 1999), pp. 221–3.

3. Joshua Trachtenberg, *Jewish Magic and Superstition* (New York 1939).

4. Moshe Rosman, *Founder of Hasidism: A Quest for the Historical Ba'al Shem Tov* (Berkeley, CA 1996), p. 56.

5. Mordkhe Kosover, *Yidishe Makholin: A shtudye in kultur-geshikhte un Shprakhn Forshung* [Jewish Food: A Study in Cultural History and Language Research] (New York 1958), pp. 129–30.

6. Pauline Wengeroff, *Rememberings: the World of a Russian Jewish Woman in the 19th Century* (College Park, MD 2000).

7. S.M. Ginsburg and P.S. Marek, *Yiddish Folksongs in Russia* (repr. Ramat Gan, IL 1991).

8. T. Sobczak, *Przełom w konsumpcji spożywczej w Królestwie Polskim w XIX wieku* (Wrocław 1968), pp. 53–9.

9. Yaffa Eliach, *There Once Was A World: A 900 Year Chronicle of the Shtetl of Eishyshok* (New York 1998), p. 289.

10. Ruth Wisse (ed.), *The I.L. Peretz Reader* (New York 1990).

11. The nineteenth-century Polish economist Wawrzyniec Surowiecki is quoted as saying just this by Ignacy Schiper in his book *Dzieje Handlu Żydowskiego na Ziemiach Polskich* (Warsaw 1937). The contemporary historian Gershon David Hundert puts forward a similar argument in his book *The Jews in a Polish Private Town – The Case of Opatów in the Eighteenth Century* (Baltimore, MD and London 1992).

12. Dr Yom Tov Lewinsky, 'The cobbler, the tailor and the baker', *Pinkasa Kehelot Polin* Vol. 91, 1964.

13. Y. Furman, 'Terminologye fun bekerfakh banitst in Bukovine un Mizrekh-Galitsye' [Terminology of the baking profession in Bukowina and Eastern Galicia], *Yidishe Shprakh* Vol. 33, 1974, pp. 32–7.

14. Written mostly by Holocaust survivors, the memorial books often contain valuable reminiscences of the ordinary people who populated a given town. Historians warn, however, that this information must be treated with some caution. Human memory is selective, especially when evoked after the violent enormity of the Holocaust.

15. Cited in Diane K. Roskies and David G. Roskies, *The Shtetl Book, An Introduction to East European Jewish Life and Lore* (Hoboken, NJ 1975).

16. Kosover, *Yidishe Makholin*, pp. 129–130.

17. Joachim Schoenfeld, *Shtetl Memoirs: Jewish Life in Galicia and in Reborn Poland 1898–1939* (Hoboken, NJ 1985).

18. Michael Galas, 'Inter-Religious Contacts in the Shtetl: Proposals for Future Research', in Antony Polonsky (ed.), *Polin* Vol. 17 *The Shtetl: Myth and Reality* (Oxford, 2004) pp. 41–50.

19. Maria Brzezina, *Polszczyzna Żydów* (Warsaw 1986), p. 53.

20. For an interesting discussion of the parallels between Jewish and non-Jewish cultural practices in Poland, see Moshe Rosman, *How Jewish is Jewish History?* (Oxford 2007). One of the examples Rosman gives is of 'festive-style, central European braided white bread [which] became the definition of *halah* for Jews in Europe and then [. . .] was polonized as *chalka* by Poles'. 'Authenticity,' Rosman observes, 'is dependent not on pedigree, but on practice.' (p. 143).

21. Ruth Wisse (ed.), *The I.L. Peretz Reader* (New York 1990), p. 277.
22. From the Działoszyc Memorial Book or *Sefer Yizkor Shel Kehilat Działoszyce ve-ha-seviva* (Tel Aviv 1973), kindly translated on the www.JewishGen website.
23. Regina Lilienthal, *Dziecko Żydowskie* [The Jewish Child] (Kraków 1927), pp. 73–4.
24. From Alexander Granach, *Eight Chapters about Horodenka*, translated from the Yiddish *Ot Gait a Mensch* on the JewishGen website.
25. I am indebted to Daniel Soyer and Jocelyn Cohen for allowing me to consult their translations of a YIVO autobiographical essay competition from 1942 which included Bertha Fox's contribution. A selection of these essays has recently been published in *My Future Is America: Autobiographies of East European Jewish Immigrants* (New York 2005).
26. Henry Tobias, *The Jewish Bund in Russia – From its Origins to 1905* (Stanford, CA 1972), p. 222.
27. Dovid Katz, *Words On Fire: The Unfinished Story of Yiddish* (New York 2004).
28. Nathan Ausubel (ed.), *A Treasury of Jewish Folklore* (New York 1948).
29. Elezier Shtaynbarg, *The Jewish Book of Fables* (Syracuse, NY 2003).

Chapter 4 Bagel Polemics in an Independent Poland

1. Ezra Mendelsohn, 'Interwar Poland: good for the Jews or bad for the Jews?', in Chimen Abramsky *et al.* (ed.), *The Jews in Poland* (Oxford 1986).
2. From the 1931 census cited by Norman Davies in *God's Playground* (New York 1982), p. 404.
3. Cited in Joseph Ansell, *Arthur Szyk – Artist, Jew, Pole* (Oxford 2004).
4. I. Bornstein, *Rzemiosło Żydowskie w Polsce* (Warsaw 1936).
5. The information about the Beigels and quotes from them are all taken from interviews conducted by the author with surviving members of the family in New York and Israel.
6. Ignacy Schiper, *Dzieje Handlu Żydowskiego na Ziemiach Polskich* (Warsaw 1937), p. 618.
7. Rafal Mahler, 'A Survey of the Jewish Bagel Pedlars of Warsaw' (in Yiddish), *Economic Life*, Vols 1–2, 1935.
8. Bernard Goldshteyn, *20 Yor in Varshever Bund* (New York 1960), reprinted in *Dos amolike Yidishe Varshe* (Montreal 1966), pp. 189–90.
9. A comparison based on official statistics in the *Mały Rocznik Statystyczny* of 1937.

10. G. Schneider (ed.), *Mordechai Gebirtig, His Poetic and Musical Legacy* (Westport, CT 2000), p. 63. Reproduced with permission of Greenwood Publishing Group, Inc., Westport, CT.

11. Wanda Wasilewska, *Prawda o Anty-semityzmie* (Warsaw 1936); cited in Celia Heller, *On the Edge of Destruction: Jews of Poland between the Two World Wars* (New York 1980).

12. Irena Krzywicka, 'W Sądzie Grodzkim', *Wiadomości Literackie* 18 March 1934.

13. Ron Nowicki, *Warsaw: The Cabaret Years* (San Francisco 1992).

14. I am indebted to both Sian Glaessner and Gerard McBurney for helping me track down the beginning of the story of 'Bublitchki'. Once the song crossed the Atlantic it became a popular fixture, played by Benny Goodman and sung by the Andrews Sisters.

15. Marta A. Balińska and William Schneider (eds), *The Story of One Life* by Ludwik Hirszfeld (Rochester, NY, forthcoming).

16. Yisrael Gutman, *The Jews of Warsaw 1939–1945* (Brighton 1982).

17. Mary Berg, *Dziennik z Getta Warszawskiego* (Warsaw 1983), p. 57.

18. Joseph Ansell, *Arthur Szyk – Artist, Jew, Pole* (Oxford 2000).

Chapter 5 Boiling Over

1. Abraham Cahan, *Yekl – A Tale of the New York Ghetto* (New York 1896).

2. Moses Rischin, *The Promised City: New York's Jews 1870–1914* (Cambridge, MA 1962), p. 67.

3. Moses Rischin (ed.), *Grandma Never Lived in America. The New Journalism of Abraham Cahan* (Bloomington, IN 1985), p. 386.

4. *Ibid.*, p. 89.

5. Rischin, *The Promised City*, p. 57.

6. Hyam Plumka was a contestant in a 1942 YIVO essay competition about life for immigrants in America. A selection of these translated essays appears in Jocelyn Cohen and Daniel Soyer (eds), *My Future is America: Autobiographies of East European Jewish Immigrants* (New York 2005). Plumka's essay was translated exclusively for the present book.

7. Plumka went on to become a street cleaner and trade union leader. He retired to California where he achieved a measure of fame, featuring in Ripley's 'Believe It Or Not' cartoon series for having written – aged 75 and virtually blind – his life story in 4,000 characters on the back of a penny postcard.

8. The building that housed Rosner's is gone, but in the early twenty-first century the same street corner is still known as a place where itinerant

labourers (now mostly Chinese) gather in the early mornings to be picked up for odd jobs.

9. A wealth of information about the formation of the Jewish bakers' labour movement is to be found in Paul Brenner, 'The Formative Years of the Hebrew Bakers' Unions 1881–1914', in *YIVO Annual of Jewish Social Science* Vol. 18, 1983, pp. 39–121.

10. Morris Hillquit, *Loose Leaves from a Busy Life* (New York 1934), p. 25.

11. *Bakers' Journal*, 31 May 1890.

12. The union officially became the Journeymen Bakers' and Confectioners' International Union in 1890.

13. *Bakers' Journal*, 25 October 1890.

14. Bernard Weinstein, *Di Idishe Yunyons in Amerika* (New York 1929).

15. *New York Press*, 30 September 1894.

16. Paul Kens, *Lochner v. New York – Economic Regulation on Trial* (Lawrence, KS 1998).

17. AG was another contestant in the 1942 YIVO essay competition.

18. Goldstein, quoted in Brenner, 'The Formative Years'.

19. *Bakers' Journal*, 26 June 1909.

20. Special Quorum, 6 February 1911; from the Archives of the B & C International, held in the Special Collections of the Hornbake Library, University of Maryland.

Chapter 6 'Kings of the Line'

1. The *Jewish Bakers' Voice* was the journal of the bakery owners. This article is taken from the issue dated 27 July 1928.

2. *Jewish Bakers' Voice*, 1948.

3. It is interesting to note that after 1945, bagel baking was usually undertaken from Thursday to Sunday, including work on the Jewish Sabbath.

4. 'Yox' were the laughs and also supplied a pun with 'lochs' (lox) or the smoked fish (salmon) eaten with bagels.

5. In researching this chapter, the author spoke to seven former members of Local 338, as well as to two of their former lawyers. She also consulted the archives of the B & C which are located in the Special Collections of the University of Maryland's Hornbake Library and the papers of the B & C's Local 3 (at New York University's Robert F. Wagner Labor Archives) with which Local 338 would merge in 1971. Unfortunately, however, the box file

containing the papers of Local 338 before 1971 has been missing in the stacks of the Wagner Archives for some six years.

6. Robert F. Kennedy, *The Enemy Within* (New York 1960).

7. For a comprehensive overview of the history of the B & C, see Stuart Bruce Kaufman, *A Vision of Unity – The History of the Bakery and Confectionary Workers International Union* (Champaign, IL 1987).

8. *Jewish Bakers' Voice*, 28 February 1958.

9. So concerned were the authorities at probable mob infiltration of various businesses that they commissioned an official investigation. The New York State Commission of Investigation 1969 report, 'An Investigation of Racketeer Infiltration into Legitimate Business', devotes 14 of its 112 pages to 'the bagel business'.

10. Trial Examiner's Decision of Case nos 1–CA–5054 and 1–CA–5165 before the National Labor Relations Board, Division of Trial Examiners, Washington, DC, 3 March 1966. Report held in the B & C Papers at the University of Maryland's Hornbake Library.

11. Author's interview with George Newman, October 2003.

12. *Christian Science Monitor*, 7 September 1971.

13. It was in 1972, for example, that H & H Bagels, a bakery destined to become a New York City cultural landmark, was opened by a Puerto Rican, Helmer Toro.

Chapter 7 The 'Bagelising' of America

1. According to the *American Jewish Yearbook*.

2. Quoted in *Frozen Food Age*'s comprehensive piece on the Lenders' story; see Warren Thayer, 'Marking 30 years in Frozens, Lender's renews quest to bagelize America. How an Immigrant Family made it and what it took – besides an ethnic recipe', June 1992.

3. The *Jewish Bakers' Voice*, 1 November 1935.

4. Author's interview with Ron Winarick, 2007.

5. These sales figures and most of the other Lender financial data quoted are derived from interviews with the Lenders. The financial records seem to have been lost.

6. Other bagel-shaping machines were developed, but the general consensus is that Thompson led the way.

7. The author interviewed Marvin Lender on three separate occasions between 2003 and 2007. Additional information was gained from

interviews with the Lenders' former creative director, Willy Evans, sales director, Barry Ansel, and financial director, Doris Zelinsky.

8. Apparently, at the time $1 bought eighteen Lenders' bagels as against five freshly baked ones.

9. Author's interview with Jules Rose, 2007.

10. *New York Times*, 24 July 1969.

11. According to one survey, 93 per cent of American households owned a toaster in 1970 as against only 21 per cent in Western Europe. Cited in Richard Tedlow, *New and Improved: The Story of Mass Marketing in America* (New York 1990).

12. *Harford Courant*, 18 May 1969.

13. Interview with Ozzie Goldman, 20 March 2007; see also Chapter 10, 'El Al Looks into the Bagel', in Arnold Sherman, *The El Al Story* (Brighton 1972).

14. Molly Goldberg and Myra Waldo, *The Molly Goldberg Cookbook* (New York 1955).

15. Milton Berle, *Milton Berle's Private Joke File* (New York 1989), p. 78.

16. *Newsweek*, 25 September 1967.

17. Author's interviews with Judith Hope Blau, 25 June and 20 March 2007.

18. *Christian Science Monitor*, 12 December 1972.

19. Mimi Sheraton, 'The Bagel Finagle', *New York* magazine, 1973.

20. Mimi Sheraton, *New York Times*, 28 March 1981.

21. From George B. Balach, 'Mattoon Queen of the Prairie' (1886); cited in Jean Johnston *et al.*, *Mattoon: A Pictorial History* (St Louis, MO 1988).

22. The author attended Mattoon's Bagelfest in July 2004 and interviewed a wide cross section of Mattooners.

Postscript

1. In spring 2007 Blackstone sold a nine per cent stake in the company to the Chinese government.

2. As home to the biggest Jewish community in Canada, Montreal would have had dozens of bakers in the early twentieth century and it is highly likely they would have been producing bagels from the start. There is documentary evidence for the existence of other bagel bakeries in Montreal in the 1930s in strike fliers printed in the *Jubilee Publication for the Jewish Bakers' Union of Montreal* (Montreal, 1938). Circumstantial evidence for this argument comes from Louis Rosenberg's *Canada's Jews: A Social And Economic Study of Jews in Canada in the 1930s* (Montreal

1939, repr. 1993, p. 180), in which he points out that there were 203 Jewish bakers in Canada in 1931, at a time when Montreal had the country's largest Jewish community.

3. The author visited Montreal and interviewed both Joe Moreno of St Viateur and Irwin Schlafman of Fairmount.

4. Donald Bell, *Saturday Night at the Bagel Factory and Other Montreal Stories* (Toronto 1972).

5. 'Oui, Grand Bagels, Non?', *Washington Post*, 11 July 1984.

6. Israel Zangwill, *Children of the Ghetto* (Detroit 1998), p. 61.

7. From 'London Lirik', 1940. I am indebted to Barry Davis for drawing my attention to this poem and for translating it into English.

8. For an informative essay on Stencl's life and work, see Dovid Katz, 'Stencl of Whitechapel', *Mendele Review*, Vol. 7, no. 003.

9. Barnet Litvinoff, *Commentary*, Vol. 10, no. 4, October 1950.

10. Note the use of 'beigel', which when pronounced is closer in sound to the Yiddish than 'bagel'.

11. Steven Berkoff, *My Life in Food* (York 2007), p. 34.

12. *Ibid.*, pp. 37–8.

13. Arthur Hertzberg, *A Jew in America* (San Francisco 2002), p. 442.

14. Irving Howe, *World of Our Fathers* (New York 1976), pp. 619–20.

15. Stanley Regelson, 'The Bagel: Symbol and Ritual at the Breakfast Table', in Susan P. Montague and W. Arens, *The American Dimension: Cultural Myths and Social Realities* (Sherman Oaks, CA 1981).

16. New Year 1999/5760 sermon by Rabbi Joshua Hammerman of Temple Beth El, Stamford Connecticut.

FURTHER READING

This is not a comprehensive list of the books consulted in the course of my research; rather, it is a selection of those specialist books in English which I found particularly useful and often thought-provoking.

On food, bread and Jewish cooking

E. N. Anderson, *The Food of China* (New Haven 1988)

John Cooper, *Eat and Be Satisfied: A Social History of Jewish Food* (Northvale, NJ 1993)

Maria Dembińska and William Weaver, *Food and Drink in Medieval Poland* (Philadelphia, PA 1999)

H.E. Jacobs, *Six Thousand Years of Bread* (New York 1997, repr. of 1944 edn)

Harold McGee, *McGee on Food & Cooking: An Encyclopedia of Kitchen Science, History and Culture* (London 2004)

Gillian Riley, *The Oxford Companion to Italian Food* (New York and Oxford 2007)

Claudia Roden, *The Book of Jewish Food: An Odyssey from Samarkand and Vilna to the Present Day* (London 1996)

Mimi Sheraton, *The Bialy Eaters: The Story of a Bread and a Lost World* (New York 2000)

R.E.F. Smith and David Christian, *Bread and Salt: A Social and Economic History of Food and Drink in Russia* (Cambridge 1984)

Robert Sternberg, *Yiddish Cuisine: A Gourmet's Approach to Jewish Cooking* (Northvale, NJ 1995)

Jan Sobieski and the Battle of Vienna

Bernard Connor, *History of Poland* (London 1698)
François Paulin Dalerac, *Polish Manuscripts of the Secret Histories of the Reign of John Sobieski* (London 1700)
Norman Davies, *Sobieski's Legacy: Polish History 1683–1983. A Lecture* (London 1985)
John Stoye, *The Siege of Vienna* (Edinburgh 2006)

Jewish history in Europe and Polish–Jewish relations

Chimen Abramsky, Maciej Jachimczyk and Antony Polonsky, *The Jews in Poland* (Oxford 1986)
Joseph P. Ansell, *Arthur Szyk: Artist, Jew, Pole* (Oxford 2004)
Itzik Gottesman, *Defining the Yiddish Nation: the Jewish Folklorists of Poland* (Detroit 2003)
Yisrael Gutman, *The Jews of Warsaw 1939–1943: Ghetto, Underground, Revolt* (Brighton 1982)
Aleksander Hertz, *The Jews in Polish Culture* (Chicago 1988)
Eva Hoffman, *Shtetl: The History of a Small Town and an Extinguished World* (London 1997)
Gershon David Hundert, *The Jews in a Polish Private Town: The Case of Opatów in the Eighteenth Century* (Baltimore, MD and London 1992)
Jacob R. Marcus, *Jews in the Medieval World* (Cincinnati 1999)
S.L. Pentlin (ed.), *The Diary of Mary Berg: Growing Up in the Warsaw Ghetto* (Oxford 2007)
Antony Polonsky *et al.* (eds), *The Jews in Old Poland 1000–1795* (Oxford 1993)
Antony Polonsky (ed.), *Polin: Studies in Polish Jewry*, published since 1987. *Polin* is an annual compedium of indispensable scholarship on Polish–Jewish history.
Moshe Rosman, *How Jewish is Jewish History?* (Oxford 2007)
Yuri Slezkine, *The Jewish Century* (Princeton, NJ 2004)

A good introduction to the *yizkhorbukh* or 'memorial books' is Jack Kugelmass and Jonathan Boyarin, *From a Ruined Garden: the Memorial Books of Polish*

Jewry (New York 1983). Many more memorial books are now available to be read in English online, thanks to the translations done by volunteers for www.Jewishgen.org.

Yiddish language and literature

Dovid Katz, *Words on Fire: The Unfinished Story of Yiddish* (New York 2004)

Eliezer Shtanybarg, *The Jewish Book of Fables* (Syracuse, NY 1983)

Ruth R. Wisse, *The I.L. Peretz Reader* (New York 1990)

Jewish history in America, particularly New York

Jocelyn Cohen and Daniel Soyer, *My Future is in America: Autobiographies of East European Jewish Immigrants* (New York 2005)

Hasia Diner, Jeffrey Shander and Beth S. Wenger (eds), *Remembering the Lower East Side* (Bloomington, IN 2000)

Lawrence Epstein, *The Haunted Smile: The Story of Jewish Comedians in America* (New York 2001)

Henry Feingold, *The Jewish People in America: A Time for Searching. Entering the Mainstream (1920–1945)* (Baltimore, MD and London 1992)

Arthur Hertzberg, *A Jew in America: My Life and a People's Struggle for Identity* (San Francisco 2002)

Irving Howe, *The World of Our Fathers* (New York 1976)

Irving Howe and Kenneth Libo, *How We Lived: A Documentary History of Immigrant Jews in America* (New York 1979)

Moses Rischin, *The Promised City: New York's Jews 1870–1914* (Cambridge, MA 1977)

Moses Rischin (ed.), *Grandma Never Lived in America: The New Journalism of Abraham Cahan* (Bloomington, IN 1985)

Richard F. Shephard and Vicki Gold Levin, *Live and Be Well: A Celebration of Yiddish Culture in America* (Piscataway, NJ 2000)

Daniel Soyer, *Jewish Immigrant Associations and American Identity in New York 1880–1939* (Cambridge, MA 1997)

Leon Stein, Abraham P. Conan and Lynn Davison (trs), *The Education of Abraham Cahan* (Philadelphia, PA 1969)

American union history

Paul Brenner, 'Formative Years in the Hebrew Bakers' Union 1881–1914', *YIVO Annual of Jewish Social Studies*, Vol. 18, 1983
Walter Galenson, *The American Labor Movement 1955–95* (Westport, CT 1996)
Morris Hillquit, *Loose Leaves from a Busy Life* (New York 1934)
Stuart Bruce Kaufman, *A Vision of Unity: the History of the Bakery and Confectionary Workers' International Union* (Urbana, IL 1986)
Elias Tcherikower, *The Early Jewish Labor Movement in the United States* (New York 1961)

The sociology of consumption and the food business in America

Warren Belasco and Philip Scranton (eds), *Food Nations: Selling Taste in Consumer Societies* (New York 2002)
Marilyn Halter, *Shopping for Identity: the Marketing of Ethnicity* (New York 2000)
Andrew Heinze, *Adapting to Abundance: Jewish Immigrants, Mass Consumption and the Search for American Identity* (New York 1980)
John and Karen Hess, *The Taste of America* (Champaign, IL 1977; reissued 2000)
Richard Tedlow, *New and Improved: The History of Mass Marketing in America* (Cambridge, MA 1996)

For children

Judith Hope Blau, *The Bagel Baker of Milliner Lane* (New York 1974)
Frances and Ginger Park and Grace Lin, *Where on Earth is My Bagel?* (New York 2001)
Daniel Pinkwater, *The Frankenbagel Monster* (New York 1986)
Ellen Schwartz and Stefan Czernecki, *Mr Belinsky's Bagels* (London and Vancouver 1997)
Robert Sebbo, *Bagel Mouse* (New York 1995)
Natasha Wing and Robert Casilla, *Jalapeno Bagels* (New York 1996)

I could not end this list without highlighting some of the books which have been written specifically about bagels – how to make them and how to eat them as well as about 'bagel lore'. Nao Hauser and Sue Spitler started the trend in 1979 with *Bagels! Bagels! And More Bagels!: A Saga of Good Eating with Recipes, Legend and Lore* (with an introduction by Murray Lender). Marilyn Bagel wrote her first book on bagels, *Bagels' Bagel Book*, in 1985: the third edition of her second book, *The Bagel Bible for Bagel Lovers*, came out in 1998. *Bagels* by Eric Friedler and Peter Loewy (Münich 1999) is a small coffee table book with photographs of New York bagel shops.

INDEX